MIKE "ASH" ASHBURN
with STEVE DUIN
foreword by DENNY RYDBERG

The Amazing Love Story

Young Life Communications
P.O. Box 520
Colorado Springs, CO 80901
(719) 381-1800

Printed in the United States of America
ISBN 0-9770338-0-5

Dedication ...

I dedicate this book to God,
and all the wonderful things
He might accomplish through it.

To my children,
Melissa, Megan, Morgan and Michael.
You are the joy of my life, and I am so very proud of you.

To my loving wife, Eva,
I'd be nothing without you. You are my
best friend and the love of my life.

Acknowledgements ...

A very special thanks:

David and Jean Spence, thank you for showing me the world and planting the seeds of this dream.

Steve Duin, thanks for believing in me and putting legs on this dream. You poured your life into this … thank you, thank you, thank you!

Young Life, who is dedicated to sharing this amazing love story with every teenager, everywhere, for eternity. I am so proud to be a part of the Young Life family. You are my "family," heroes of the faith … keep encouraged!

Denny Rydberg, the president of Young Life, thanks for having the vision to lead our mission, and the grace to "turn me loose" to use my gifts.

All the folks in the Young Life Communications Services department.

Keri Stephens, thank you so much for the hours you put in as my personal English teacher and transcriber. You and your precious family are so dear to us!

Marion Chesney and her Daddy, for inspiring the story of "Here I am, Daddy." I'm so glad you were such a terrible hider … that you liked to hide … but loved to be found.

Mom and Dad, for raising me to chase after big things.

Tim, my brother, thanks for letting me tag along. I've watched you closely … you have paved the way for me in ways that you would never imagine.

Table of Contents

Foreword

Today is not like every other day. First, it's not every day that you pick up a book, open it and discover that it's actually written about you. But that's the case with the book that you hold in your hands. It's a story about you, about someone who loves you and about an adventure waiting to be lived! And second, it's not every day that you meet a character like the man who wrote this book.

You may have never met Mike "Ash" Ashburn before, but I believe you'll soon feel like he's an old friend. Ash is the kind of friend you could talk to for hours, or sit for a long time and say nothing and still feel heard and understood. One thing you might not know about Ash, he's a living legend in Young Life. He travels the country and the world talking with kids and adults at camps, conferences and other events. People love to listen because few people can tell a story like Mike Ashburn. And the story he is telling in this book is the greatest story ever told. It's the story of a kind and generous God pursuing you with His wild and disarming love.

Ash tells the story just like you might hear it told at Young Life camp or in club. He uses colorful pictures and clear language to offer simple information to consider about the most important stuff in life: relationships, faith, hope, love. It's a story worth repeating, worth re-reading, worth considering and discussing with your Young Life leaders and friends. I hope you will see yourself in this story and discover something worth remembering forever.

Denny Rydberg
President, Young Life

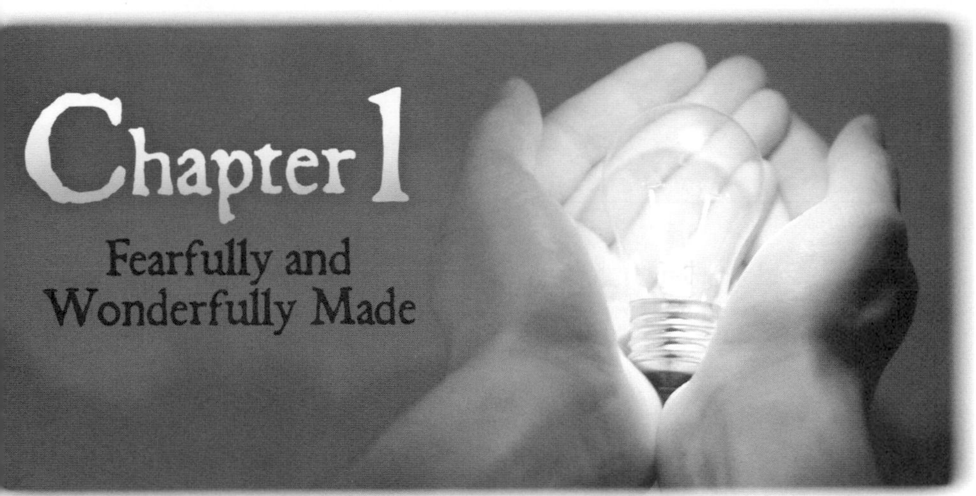

Chapter 1
Fearfully and Wonderfully Made

This is a story first told to me on the front porch of my Granny's house, deep in the hills of Tennessee. I was a little boy then, but the story has carried me from that porch to where I am today.

When I was growing up, Granny felt the same way about adventure as I did. After playing hide-and-seek in the cornfields, exploring caves, skinning catfish or shooting rats at a nearby dump — how's that for adventure! — Granny and I would catch our breath on the old porch swing.

I was usually exhausted on those quiet, humid nights. Granny was just soft enough to snuggle up against. And as we sat together in the fading light, the swing gently squeaking beneath us, Granny unfolded the story that I want to pass along to you.

I cherish the memory of those nights. It was a chance to slow down ... and take a long look at life. That doesn't happen very often. There aren't many opportunities to think about what it all means. To ask questions like: "Who am I?"

"Why am I here?'

Questions like: "Is there a God?"

"And what does that have to do with me?"

That's where I come in. I consider myself the luckiest man alive at the moment. Because I've been handed the microphone, so to speak, so that I can share with you the Amazing Love Story. It's a true story. It's a story about God and Jesus and you.

I'll make a deal with you. I want you to understand that while I can't see your face or guess your weight or know everything going on in your life, I accept you just the way you are. I'm not asking you to change. I have no interest in frightening you. I don't even mind if you keep the iPod going in the background. All I want is a little of your time … so you can decide for yourself if this love story makes sense. And I'll give you everything I've got. I'll try real hard to tell it just the way it is. I'll be careful not to add anything to it or take anything away from it.

I don't know how you'll receive this love story. The Bible is packed with stories about how others responded. There was, for example, a guy named Zacchaeus. Nobody liked him. He was a tax collector. He was real short and didn't have much going for him. He didn't know very much about Jesus, but on the day Jesus came through town, Zacchaeus noticed that everyone was hanging around Him. Zacchaeus was curious about that, so this is what he did: He ran way up ahead of the parade and climbed a sycamore tree, reaching for a better view. He crawled way out on a limb, which was pretty risky. My hope and prayer for you — in the hours or days that you spend with this book — is that you will at least do that. That you will risk just enough to climb out on a limb, maybe for the first time in your life, to get a really good look at this guy. At Jesus Christ.

There was another guy in the Bible. Nicodemus. He was so afraid about what his friends might think that he went to see Jesus at night, on the sly, so that no one else would know about it. I only mention Nicodemus because you might like that approach. You may be tempted to avoid the crowd, to keep the drapes pulled on your curiosity, to sneak up on the man. If you feel like that, that's OK.

I want it to be really easy for you to check Jesus out. Because you never know. You may be like Peter. His response to the Amazing Love Story was to jump in with both feet. He dropped everything in his life and became a follower of Christ. I'd be lying if I pretended that wasn't my hope for you. Because I know a few guys like Nathaniel will also pick up this book. Nathaniel's response to Jesus, at least in the beginning, was, "You've got to be kidding me. No, thanks. I don't want to have anything to do with this Jesus of Nazareth." You know what? If that's your response, I won't love you any less. But … you knew there was a "but" coming, didn't you? But … the really wild truth is this: Neither will God.

This Amazing Love Story — this story about God and Jesus and you — begins in the Bible. Now, when you pick up that Bible — and don't worry if you don't happen to have one around — the very first page (once you get past all the maps and the table of contents) pretty much sums up how God intended things to be between you and Him. His intentions are laid out pretty clearly in the first two pages of Genesis.

But on the very next page, in Genesis 3, something terrible happened. It was so tragic, so devastating, so gross, that it changed everything. It changed the course of human history. Nothing that has happened since compares to the tragedy in that chapter.

You need to imagine that Bible for a moment. You have the book sitting there in your right hand. You've opened it up to the third chapter of Genesis, so you have this tiny portion of the Bible — what, two pages? — on the left side and the rest of a pretty thick book on the right side.

Can you picture that? I hope so. Because while those two pages on the left are the story of what God built in the beginning and how it broke down, everything on the right — the rest of that big, honkin' Bible — is the story of what God did to fix things. Why? Because that's how much He loves you.

It's an Amazing Love Story. It starts with the idea that you are no cosmic accident. In fact, it begins with the idea that you were created for a purpose. Now, when I talk about "you," I'm not talking about a group of you. I'm not talking about the sophomores or the Methodists or everyone from Tennessee. I'm talking about YOU individually. The Amazing Love Story begins with the idea that you were created for the distinct purpose of being in a relationship with the God who created you.

You know what I hate about our world today? You are among the sharpest group of teenagers in human history … and our society treats you like idiots. And society has lied to you. Lied to you so convincingly, I guess, that many of us buy into the lies that don't mesh with the Amazing Love Story.

One of the first lies that I bought into when I was your age was that I was ordinary. You know that feeling, don't you? Let's say you're a teenage girl. You're at the grocery store. You walk through the check-out line and glance over and there on the rack is a copy of *Cosmopolitan* magazine. And on the cover of *Cosmo* there is a perfect image of a woman's face and the perfect image of a woman's body. You look at that magazine cover for a moment or two and you say to yourself, "I don't look like that. I must be ordinary."

It's the same with the guys. You see a copy of *GQ* or *Cigar Aficionado* and there's some stud guy with his shirt half off. And his abs are rolling down the page. Guys, when I take my shirt off, my abs don't do anything. They just sit there. But we look at those magazines and we say, "I don't look like that. I must be ordinary." And I gotta tell you: That is the biggest load of dooky I've heard in my entire life.

Because the Amazing Love Story makes this really clear:

You are not ordinary.

Not even close.

You are extraordinary.

In fact, the Amazing Love Story says to you ladies: "You are princesses. You are the crown jewel of all creation." You're not ordinary.

The picture on that magazine is a lie. If that woman walked into the room right now, you wouldn't recognize her. She doesn't look like that. She'd be the first to tell you so. Before she can climb onto the cover of *Cosmo*, the photographers take hundreds, perhaps thousands, of pictures. They might fly her to an island in the Greek Isles called Santorini, where the water is unforgettably blue and the sky is perfect and the lighting is flawless. There's a makeup crew. A lighting crew. A film crew. A producer. They snap a picture of her. They freeze one millisecond of her life. And then they computer enhance it. They airbrush out all the flaws. Then they put that mirage, that utter lie, on a magazine cover, just in time for you to wander by and feel … ordinary. And that's crap. I beg you. Don't buy into the lie.

The Amazing Love Story says you were created in the image of a God who is absolutely crazy about you. God created man and woman. And the Bible says this is how He did it:

> *In the beginning God created the*
> *heavens and the earth.* Genesis 1:1
> Today's New International Version (TNIV)

You want to know how He pulled that off? He spoke all things into existence.

You have to pull out that imagination again. Everything was dark. And God — a perfect, Holy Spirit — said, "Let there be light!" And POW: The stars splashed across the night sky. God was only getting started. He said, "Let there be vegetation. And animals." He spoke them into existence, too. When He got done creating all those things, He looked down at His creation and He said, "It. Is. Good."

That's when you came along. You were so precious, you were so amazing, you were so beautiful, that when God finished creating Adam and Eve, man and woman, you and me, He was so stunned by the results that it completely changed God's perspective about His creation. When He got done with you, He

said, "It is VERY good." "Good" wasn't good enough. "Good" didn't cut it. It's not hard to see why. You are not ordinary. You are not a cosmic accident. The world is trying to convince you you're just a little higher than the apes. The Amazing Love Story says you are just a little lower than the angels!

Girls? Do you realize that you are the last thing that God made? You are His final inspiration. You are the crown jewel of His creation. You are so wonderful, so beautiful, that when God first showed you to Adam, the poor guy was dumbfounded. He was speechless. He stood there like a salt lick, not knowing what to say.

And guys? You are valiant warriors. You are not idiots. You are not rabbits that have to have sex all the time, or anything like that. You are heroes! You are men of God, created by Him and for Him.

You know those words I just suggested came bubbling out of God's mouth? The Old Testament, the first books of the Bible, is written in Hebrew. When God looked down and decided things were "very good," the Hebrew word He used is: "Tove." And when God took in His beautiful princesses and valiant warriors, He didn't whisper the word. He looked at everything in creation, at the Grand Canyon, at Niagara Falls, at the beauty of an eagle swooping out of the trees and skimming across the water … and then He looked at you and said, "No, these creatures are different." Why? Because only you are made in God's image. Nothing else in the universe can say that. He looked at you and He said: "TOVE! TOVE! TOVE! TOVE!" You are that special. You are amazing subjects of God's love.

Our movies, our magazines, our music, they teach you that you are a sexual object. But you are not. I wish I could get you to understand this. It's so important. Don't buy into the lie that you aren't special. The Amazing Love Story starts with the idea that you are fearfully and wonderfully created in the image of a God who is absolutely, head-over-heels, crazy-in-love, nuts about you … and wants to be in a relationship with you.

Several years ago, I was at a Young Life camp. I was standing at the front of a room filled with 200 teenagers and I told them everything I've told you so far. Everyone was laughing and having a good time, and in the middle of that good time, I noticed several kids were passing a note forward. This 3x5 note card was rolling up toward me, passed from one kid to the next, until it reached the front of the room. This caught me off guard. I had no idea what to expect. I opened up the note and I could tell from the handwriting that it was from a young lady. And what it said was this:

How can that be true?

You don't know me.

You don't know how dirty I am.

I turned the note card over. On the other side, she'd written, "I'm a teenage stripper." And then it said in bold, capital letters: *I AM A SLUT.*

I just stood there, that piece of paper in my hands. I had a room full of kids staring at me … and I didn't know what to say.

If you're reading this book, there may be something in your life that makes you feel just that dirty. There may be something in your life that convinces you it would be impossible for you to be loved by the God who created you. You may think you harbor some deep, dark, hidden thing that makes you feel like an untouchable before God. I want to tell you, then, what I told the kids in that room:

God loves sluts!

He is nuts about 'em. Absolutely nuts. And He is nuts about you. God loves you!

That is the heart of the Amazing Love Story.

When I was in college, my major was wildlife biology. I love science. And much of what science teaches goes right along with the Amazing Love Story, except that it leaves out the most important thing: Who initiated it all? If it turns out that the universe was created by the Big Bang, then yippee skippy. The question remains: Who lit the fuse to the Big Bang?

Evolution would have you believe that all life started, randomly, from one single cell. And that's an intriguing thought. I was on vacation once, walking along the beach, when I looked down and spotted a watch. It was gorgeous. All shiny. It looked brand new. I looked around to see if anyone was watching or if anyone was looking for it, and then I picked it up. And what do you know: It was a Swiss watch. There were jewels, and sweeping, gold hands. I began to wonder where the watch came from, and then it hit me: A gazillion years ago, I bet there was a mud puddle right here. And when the light hit it just right, this watch flopped out onto the beach. You know what? That's definitely a possibility.

But it's a lot easier for me to imagine this little bitty short guy with bushy eyebrows and this visor that comes way down and these microscope-glasses that come way out to the tip of his nose, and he's all hunkered over a bench, clutching these tweezers, paying desperate attention to every little detail because he wants to get it just right. He wants to make it perfect. Because he knows the watch is going to be an expression of himself.

I believe, folks, that each of you is like that watch. You are no cosmic accident, thrown into the night skies of chance. You are not the result of the marriage of random molecules. You are the product of a loving God who paid desperate attention to every little detail to ensure that you were fearfully and wonderfully made. He wanted you to be an expression of Himself.

No wonder the Psalmist said:

> *When I consider your heavens,*
> *the work of your fingers,*
> *the moon and the stars*
> *which you have set in place,*
> *what are mere mortals that you are*
> *mindful of them,*
> *human beings that you care for them?*
> *You have made them a little lower than*
> *the heavenly beings*
> *and crowned them with glory and honor.*
> *You made them rulers over the works of*
> *your hands;*
> *you put everything under their feet.*
> Psalm 8:3-6 (TNIV)

What are mere mortals? For each of us, I think God wants that question to be much more personal:

Who am I, Lord, that you would think of me?

Who am I that you would care for me?

Who am I to know that kind of love?

How is that possible? Once again, the Psalmist picks us up and carries us to the heart of the matter:

> *For you created my inmost being;*
> *You knit me together in my mother's womb.*
> *I praise you because I am fearfully and*
> *wonderfully made;*
> *your works are wonderful,*
> *I know that full well.*
> Psalm 139:13-14 (TNIV)

I don't know how you will respond to the Amazing Love Story. You probably don't know yet, either. But I hope that as we go along, you might be willing to pray this prayer:

> *Search me, God, and know my heart;*
> *test me and know my anxious thoughts.*
> *See if there is any offensive way in me,*
> *and lead me in the way everlasting.*
> Psalm 139:23-24 (TNIV)

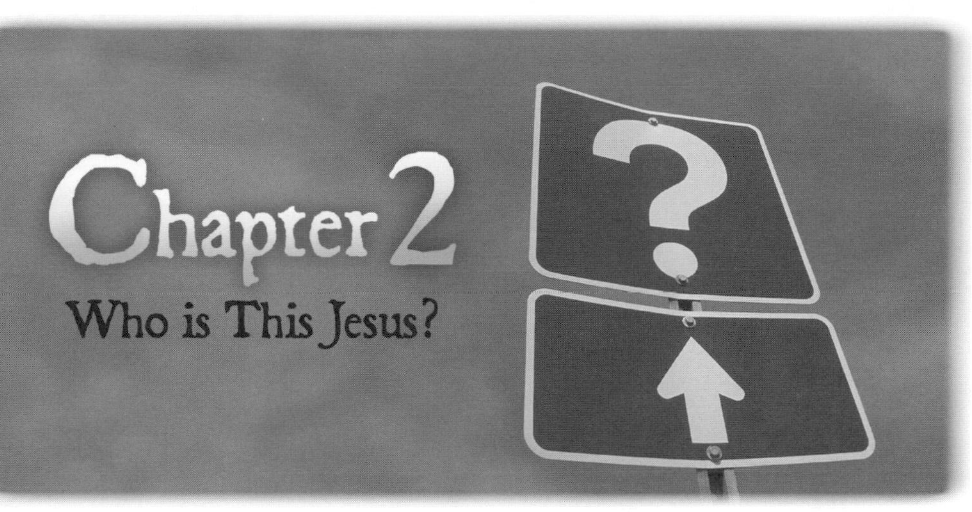

Chapter 2
Who is This Jesus?

For a moment, I want you to forget about this book. I want you to forget the chair you're curled up in or the porch you're sitting on, and I want you to remember a time in your life when you were laughing so hard that tears were running down your face. And when you looked around, probably at the friends who were laughing right along with you, you surely thought to yourself, "This is so great. Can life possibly get any better than this?" It can. I'm certain of that. I'm certain of that because I've just gotten started … with this Amazing Love Story.

You remember the last chapter, right? I trust that you're with me so far in believing this: You are not ordinary. You are extraordinary. You are no cosmic accident. You are fearfully and wonderfully made in the image of a God who is absolutely nuts in love with you. And because that is true, your purpose in life is to be in a relationship with God. God is a spirit. No one has ever seen Him. Yet this perfect and holy God has breathed life into your soul and has called you from nothingness into life.

In the first chapter of Genesis, God breathed life into this universe and into this planet. The description of life in the first two pages of the Bible is how God intended this world to be. Yet on the very next page, something terrible happened — something so terrible that it changed the course of human history. It didn't, however, change God. God didn't turn His back. God didn't walk away. God chose to fix the problem … and this is the story of how He pulled that off.

This is the part of the Amazing Love Story that absolutely changed my life. The awesome truth is there is nothing about my life today that is the same as it was before I heard the message that I'm going to share with you now. You may not know this — and I hope it doesn't freak you out — but I'm a minister. On my American Express card, it says, "Reverend Michael J. Ashburn." The reason it says that — "Reverend" — is that on the night I heard this part of the Amazing Love Story, I decided I wanted to spend the rest of my life telling as many people as possible, especially young people, the story of this amazing love.

I've been lucky. I often get to tell that story at Young Life camps across the United States and Canada. Camps like Windy Gap in North Carolina, Frontier Ranch in Colorado and Malibu Club in British Columbia. Other people who tell this story have spread the news in much wilder places, places like Colombia in South America or Kenya in Africa. Better them than me. I'm not cut out for the wild, for one reason and one reason only.

I hate snakes. They absolutely freak me out.

This is a true story: If you were a missionary or part of the Armed Forces at the end of the Second World War, you received a survivor manual when you shipped off to South America. There were chapters on how to find water and how to find food, but the showstopper in that manual was the chapter that told you what to do if you ever came across an Anaconda snake.

I have a fairly good feel for the Anaconda. My college major was wildlife biology, remember, and I once studied the snake for a term paper I was writing. The Anaconda is the largest snake in the world. It can be as big around as a basketball. Some of the snakes weigh more than 300 pounds and end up more than 30 feet long. That's three times as long as an SUV. That's longer than a lot of swimming pools. These snakes are predators. They love to choke down big animals whole. And if an Anaconda were to sneak up on you, it would treat you as just another big, dumb animal. The snake would catch you, wrap itself around you, squeeze you until you die, then swallow you whole. Which is why they got a manual about Anacondas when they went to South America.

You can picture that, can't you? You're skipping through the jungle and you look down and there's a 30-foot-long, 300-pound Anaconda, staring at you while its tongue flickers in and out. I'm sure the first thing you think to yourself is, "Thank goodness, I've got my manual!"

When you pop it open, the first thing the manual tells you is, "Don't run." Why is that? Because if you run, that sudden movement triggers an attacking instinct in the snake and it quickly catches you, squeezes you until you die and swallows you whole.

So you think to yourself, "OK, I won't run." The manual, of course, isn't going to leave you there. Step Two, it says, is "Lie down." The idea is this: If the Anaconda thinks you're dead, the snake won't wrap itself around you and squeeze you until you die.

So, there you are, lying perfectly still on the jungle floor, hoping and praying the snake will think you're dead. That's when you go to Step Three in the manual, which says, "Allow the snake to peruse your body." I love that word: *Pe-ruuuuse.* You're still lying, perfectly still, and the snake is *pe-ruuuusing* your body. And if that's not horrible enough, you go to Step Four in the manual, which says, "Allow the snake to swallow you feet first." I guess that means that if the Anaconda takes a hankerin' to your head, you're plum out of luck. But if it's at all possible, you're supposed to arrange your body so that when the snake dislocates its jaw, it swallows you, Nikes first.

So, there you are, lying on the jungle floor in South America, while a 300-pound, 30-foot snake swallows your feet, then your knees, then your hips, then slowly wraps those snake lips around your chest. About the time the snake gets to your neck and you are cocooned inside that Anaconda, things might be looking a little dark, except for this: You had the forethought to keep your manual hand out! And the last life-saving instruction about what to do if you come across an Anaconda snake? Well, the manual says, take that hand that's still at your side, grip your knife and from the inside, cut off the snake's head! The Anaconda, you see, is completely vulnerable when you're stuck in its throat. The sucker has its mouth full. All you gotta do, real quick, is — *fffffttttt* — slit his throat, severing his spinal cord, and the snake is dead instantly. Then you literally crawl out of a dead snake.

Pretty slick, huh? But imagine how scary it would be if you got to that last, vital step and you found yourself saying: *"Knife? What knife?"*

You see, all the rules about what you do when you come across an Anaconda snake — on how to survive in the wild — are dependent on one thing: You need a knife. If you don't have a knife, none of those instructions makes sense. You'd be far better off just to run.

Most of us live in a different jungle. We confront a different set of snakes. And I have to tell you: In my life, my knife is Jesus Christ. Without Him, nothin' else makes sense. All the rules of life are upside-down, topsy-turvy. They're complete nonsense. Without Jesus, I'd be better off to just wander off and live life on my own. Jesus makes God personal. I'll say that again: Jesus makes God personal.

I need to explain that. You probably have questions. When you hear me talking about God and Jesus, you may be asking, "Who are they? What's the difference between God and Jesus?" As I said earlier, God is a spirit. No one has ever seen that spirit. The person who probably got the closest was a guy named Moses, and he asked the same question that you and I would ask: *"God, everyone wants to see you. Who do I tell them that you are?"* And God said, *"Tell them that I AM."* Then God told Moses to go and hide behind a rock so that God could reveal as much of Himself as possible to him.

Look, I don't understand this completely, but the Bible suggests that a holy God can't come into contact with man. God is so pure and so off-the-charts wonderful that His radiance — His holiness, I guess you'd call it — would obliterate the human being who stood in His shadow. Because God had no intention of obliterating Moses, He only showed Moses His back. Moses just got the briefest glimpse of God's glory.

I've called this a love story. An Amazing Love Story. I want you to understand the shape of it. When God created you, He knew there would come an evening when you would look up into the night sky and say, "You know what? I'd love to believe in you, but I can't see you. I can't touch you. *"God, where are you?"*

Do you know what keeps *me* up at night? The possibility that you don't understand God has answered the question. In our last chapter, we talked about what happened at the dawn of time. God spoke this world into existence. He said, "Let there be light," and light appeared. God's words, God's command, caused light — and all the creatures in the sea, on the Earth and in the heavens — to come into existence. God's word — and in Greek, "word" means *logo* — became flesh. The Apostle John described it like this:

> *In the beginning was the Word, and the Word was with God, and the Word was God.*
> John 1:1 (TNIV)

Now, what does that mean? Well, "Word" means logo … and I know you've heard all about logos. A logo is a symbol, a symbol that's incredibly powerful and significant in our world. In fact, if a company has a really cool logo, you don't need to look any further than the logo to understand something about that company. If I held up the Golden Arches, I wouldn't have to say "McDonald's." You'd hear the word and probably see the drive-thru window. If I held up that logo to your parents, I wouldn't have to say, "Two all-beef patties, special sauce, lettuce, cheese, pickle, onion on a sesame-seed bun." They'd still hear the jingle. If I held up the swoosh, I wouldn't have to say, "Nike," or "Just do it." You'd hear both of them. And with Nike's logo, it's more than that. You don't just think Nike. You see the Nike athletes. You see Michael Jordan or Tiger Woods. You come up with a person who is identified and represented by that logo.

OK, so let's try one more. I want you to take a deep breath, clear your head and imagine what you think Jesus Christ looks like. Hold on to that image. Because Jesus is God's logo. He's God's perfect logo. And the idea is this: You need look no further than Jesus Christ to know *everything* there is to know about the God who created you. The absolute truth is that Jesus is God … in the flesh.

In Genesis, you remember, God said, *"Let there be light,"* and there was light. God said, *"Let there be trees,"* and suddenly there were oaks and sycamores and ponderosa pines. But when you came along, it was different. It had to be. God was working on something extraordinary. Genesis 1:26 (TNIV) records it this way:

> *Then God said, "Let us make human beings in our image, in our likeness."*

You are so special because you are the only one who bears the likeness of God. But who is "us"? It's God and Jesus, somehow coexisting together. Remember those words in John 1? *"In the beginning was the Word, and the Word was with God, and the*

Word was God." You could just as easily say it like this: "In the beginning was Jesus, and Jesus was with God, and Jesus was God." A little later John puts it this way:

> *The Word became flesh and made his dwelling among us. We have seen his glory, the glory of the one and only Son, who came from the Father, full of grace and truth.* John 1:14 (TNIV)

Jesus is God in the flesh. Colossians 1:15 says that Jesus is the visible expression of an unseen God. If you need a little help visualizing that, study a light bulb. The electricity that keeps that light on is the exact electricity that is outside in the wires. The light bulb is simply a form of that electricity that we can see and touch and experience. That is who Jesus Christ is. A form — a logo — of God we can see and touch and experience.

One of the great mysteries about Jesus is that He is both 100 percent God and 100 percent man. Jesus Christ is God. He was also human. He laughed, He cried, He felt joy and pain. He was 100 percent human, just like you and me, except that He was the perfect human. He was the human being that you and I were created to be. The closest analogy here on Earth as to who Jesus Christ is? I'd say it's the Bible. In a wonderful, mysterious way, the Bible is 100 percent man. It was written by human fingers. Someone wrote it. Someone copied it. Someone glued the binding together. But the Bible is also 100 percent God because God was whispering in the ear of the people who wrote it. The Word became flesh and dwelt among us. As it says in Hebrews,

Jesus is *"the radiance of God's glory and the exact representation of His being"* (Hebrews 1:3 TNIV).

Let me describe it another way. Before I got married, I had these three dogs. George, Tick and Buster. They were great dogs. I lived way out in the country on this farm, and when I would go out to the front porch and call them, those dogs would come running across the pasture, barrel through the front door and crash into the living room. Then they'd hit the kitchen linoleum and start sliding, back-pedaling, rolling right into the cupboard: Bam! Bam! Bam! Finally, they'd make a hard right and gallop into the family room.

Now in the family room, I had three chairs I'd picked up at the dump, three nasty, stinky chairs. (Remember, this was way before I got married.) So those three dogs, George, Tick and Buster, would hop into their own chairs. They would park there all day. That's how I trained 'em. They would stay in those chairs all day, sleeping, chewing on fleas, watching a little *Scooby Doo.* The only exception was this: In the kitchen I had this squeaky clean apple bucket, the kind you use at Halloween when you're dunkin' for apples. I kept that apple bucket full of perfectly clean water. Changed it every night. Now, whenever they got thirsty, Buster and Tick would bounce off their chairs, stick their heads in the bucket for a drink of water, then go straight back to their assigned seats.

But George? George didn't get it. He'd roll off his chair, and march straight past the sparkling water I'd set out for him. He'd walk right into the bathroom and drink out of the toilet. It was disgusting! The sound would echo through the house. I tried everything to get him to stop. I made loud noises. I ruffled the shower curtain. I slammed the lid down on his head. But George? He would not get it. So, here's what I did. I got this great idea. It hit me like a flash: *To show this goofy dog the error of his ways … I'll become a dog!* And I did. I became a dog. I got right down in George's face and said, "Hey, buddy! Don't drink out of the toilet! If you knew what went on in there, you would not be drinking out of the toilet!"

You know what? I can't become a dog. We know that. But the God of the universe, who splashed the galaxies across the sky, and tenderly, perfectly, created you in His image, doesn't have any such limitations. God had the power to become a human being.

Two thousand years ago in the Middle East, under a night sky in Israel, shepherd boys (teenagers) were out watching their sheep. They were bored silly, wondering if there was more to life than this. They were staring into the darkness, marveling at the stars, wondering if there was a God and what in the world He might have to do with them. And there was a dazzling bright light — the star of Bethlehem, it turns out — and an angel of the Lord saying, *"Behold! I bring you good news of great joy, glad tidings for all people. Today a Savior named Jesus has been born"* (Luke 20:10, paraphrase).

You see, folks, the story of Christmas is the story of God becoming a man. It's the story of God moving into the neighborhood. Jesus, born that day, is God in the flesh. Jesus makes God personal. And now, everybody — *Yo, Moses! Yeah, you! Come on out from behind that rock!* — can see what God is like. Jesus Christ is fully human and fully God.

What was this God-man like? Come with me, for a moment,

back to the Sea of Galilee. Come with me to the edge of the water, where we find Jesus and His disciples and their boat.

> *Late that day he said to them, "Let's go across to the other side." They took him in the boat as he was. Other boats came along. A huge storm came up. Waves poured into the boat, threatening to sink it.*
> Mark 4:35-37 (The Message)

It was a boat no bigger than your bedroom, with one mast and one sail. That storm came up on the Sea of Galilee, which was small enough that you could see (just barely) from one side to the other. The disciples were smack dab in the middle of that pond when this storm came upon them, so vicious that they're latching themselves to the pole. They were terrified. A dozen big, burly guys, and they're screaming like little girls! The storm was so loud, and they were howling, "We're going to die! We're going to die!" And finally their panic was such that they crawled to the back of the boat, where Jesus was sleeping with His head on a pillow.

> *They roused him, saying, "Teacher, is it nothing to you that we're going down?" Awake now, he told the wind to pipe down and said to the sea, "Quiet! Settle down!" The wind ran out of breath; the sea became smooth as glass.* Mark 4:38-39 (The Message)

The disciples? They were staggered. They were dumbfounded. In the stillness, all you could hear was their ragged breath and the drops of water rolling off their cheeks and onto the deck. Then one of the disciples stumbled to the edge of the boat and said,

"Who is this, anyway, that even the wind and the sea obey Him?"

I have my hand up.

I'll tell you who He was.

He was God.

Jesus is God.

I want you to put this book down again, if only for a moment, and ask yourself a few questions. In your life, what is your knife? What's the one thing you need to have so that everything else in life makes sense? Then think about this: What in your life feels like toilet water? Be honest about that one. I think it will help you to recognize the clear, sparkling water I'll offer you in the pages still to come.

In our last chapter, I told you about the part of the Amazing Love Story that really grabbed me. Grabbed me to the point where I decided it would be a privilege if my job, for the rest of my life, were to tell the story of how the God of the universe, who fearfully and wonderfully created you, anticipating the day when you would look around and say, "Hey! Where are you?"

> *The word became flesh and made his dwelling among us.* John 1:14a (TNIV)

Jesus is the visible expression of an unseen God. You need look no further than Jesus Christ to discover everything you need to know about the God who created you. And that's a big help, because it's so easy to misunderstand what God is like. Some people think He's the grand scorekeeper, this old man parked up in heaven in His rocking chair, looking down on us, waiting for us to make a mistake. Each time we do, He comes up out of that chair and puts a check mark by our name. Or He's up there with a lightning bolt, which He unloads each time you do something wrong. God became a man in order to help us clear up such misconceptions.

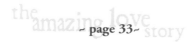

Jesus makes God personal. And the whole idea is this: If you want to have a relationship with the God who created you, you can do that face to face with Christ.

You may not be quite ready for that, though. Maybe you want to check the guy out. I mean, who was this God-man? Who was this fully-human, fully-divine character who stood up in the middle of the storm and told the wind and the sea to be still?

To be honest, we don't know very much about the first 12 years of His life. We do know that when Jesus was 12, His mother, Mary, and His earthly father, Joseph, dragged Him to a big festival in downtown Jerusalem. This festival was an annual event. When it was winding down, Mary and Joseph — who were, ordinarily, attentive parents, I have to believe — looked up and realized Jesus had disappeared. They didn't know how long He'd been gone. But when they walked back to the festival, they found Jesus in the synagogue, the local church. And you know what? He was teaching the Sunday School teachers. Everyone was sitting around scratching their heads, wondering how this kid — He was what, the equivalent of a sixth-grader today? — could be so wise in the Scripture. They didn't know that He'd written it.

Jesus. God among us. I talked earlier about our misconceptions of God, but people have some funny ideas of Jesus, too. Some people think Jesus was this wimpy, skinny, spindly guy, skipping through the desert with a sheep around His neck, saying things like, "Verily, verily, I say unto you …"

Jesus was nothing like that. Jesus was a carpenter. He was a Jew, so He probably had dark-brown or olive-colored skin. He had black eyes and, I'm guessing, long coal-black hair, maybe shoulder length, which was the common style back then. He was a common man from a common family from a little town called Nazareth. His father was a carpenter and Jesus was a carpenter's apprentice. Growing up in Joseph's house, He learned to work with wood. His toga was most likely the color of oatmeal; it was probably made out of goat's hair or something like burlap. When you stood close to Him, He smelled like sawdust or like a man who'd worked hard all day. A wimp? Please. He had calluses on His hands. He carried beams on His shoulders, beams of acacia wood, the hardest and heaviest wood known to man. And I believe that when He looked at you, you felt as if you were the only person in the world at that moment. He was very popular. People followed Him all over Judea. Everyone wanted to be with Jesus Christ, yet Scripture says He was nothing special to look at. Scripture doesn't say much at all about Jesus until He was 30 years old. That's when He began to let the world know that He was God among us.

At that point, not many were in on the secret. His mother, Mary, of course, could still hear the echo of the angel telling her she was carrying the God of the universe in her womb. Joseph knew his son was conceived by God's Holy Spirit. That allowed him to put up with the ridicule Mary endured for supposedly getting pregnant out of wedlock. But that was about it. At least, that was about it until Jesus was 30 years old and He began to reveal Himself to the world as God in the flesh. The very first time He did this was at a wedding.

Three days later there was a wedding in the village of Cana in Galilee. Jesus' mother was there. Jesus and his disciples were guests also. When they started running low on wine at the wedding banquet, Jesus' mother told him, "They're just about out of wine."
John 2:1-3 (The Message)

Now, the Bible goes on to tell us that Jesus must have given His mother quite the look. He asked the question:

"Is that any of our business, Mother — yours or mine? This isn't my time. Don't push me."
John 2:4 (The Message)

And what time is that? Time to show the world that He is God. Mary, of course, realizes that's a decision for Jesus, and she tells the servants, "Whatever He tells you, do it."

I hope you can picture this. The whole town is at this wedding. Everyone had come to the ceremony, and as each guest came through the door, they performed the same ritual. They didn't wipe their feet on the little rug or mat inside the front door, the way our moms are always asking us to do. Instead, they took their sandals off and stepped into this small bowl of water. Then they wiped their feet off with a towel, unless, of course, they were at some palace where servants would descend on them and pat their feet dry.

At this wedding, there were six huge pots of this water. Each of those pots contained about 30 gallons and the whole town had swished their feet around inside them. Can you imagine what that water must have looked like? These guests were commoners. Farmers. Sheep herders. They walked around in the desert all day and they'd left a good chunk of it in those stone pots. And that's not all. There was toe jam. Little sheep biscuits, floating around in there. I mean, it was nasty! By the time everyone was seated for the ceremony, the aroma of that water must have been pretty rich. So what does Jesus say? He tells the servants to fill those jars to the brim with water. Then He adds, "Now fill your pitchers and take them to the host."

The servants probably drew straws. I bet they were laughing their butts off. Foot water? For the boss? "Let me! Let me!" When one of the servants filled a pitcher with the stuff and walked that pitcher up to the head guy to pour him a glass, I'm sure he turned around and took off running. He didn't want to be there when the boss put that water to his lips. That's exactly what the master did. He drank it. All his servants are behind the curtains, giggling and holding their breath. And the master drinks. And sighs. And this is what he said:

> *"Everybody I know begins with their finest wines and after the guests have had their fill brings in the cheap stuff. But you've saved the best till now!"*
> John 2:10 (The Message)

"And this," the Apostle John goes on to say, *"the first of his miraculous signs, Jesus performed in Cana of Galilee. He thus revealed His glory, and His disciples put their faith in Him."*

Jesus Christ took yucky, stinkin' foot water … and He turned it into something beautiful and useful and sweet, like wine.

I hope you understand that's not just a story about foot water. It's a story about you and me. Jesus wants our foot water. You don't have to hide it from Him. The yuckiest, stinkiest, nastiest thing in your life, He can take and turn into something beautiful.

Only Jesus can do that.

He's the only one who can turn foot water into wine. He's the only one who can take the foot water of your life and turn it into a miracle.

Here's another story about Jesus: A man was walking down the road. He was scarred and disfigured by leprosy. Leprosy was a horrible skin disease. It literally stripped the flesh from your bones. It wasn't uncommon for a leper to wake up in the morning and discover that a finger had fallen off while he slept. Lepers were complete social outcasts. Everyone believed leprosy was contagious and that it was passed on by touching. Imagine if AIDS were transmitted by touching and you'll have a sense of how people in those days thought about this fatal disease. Lepers lived outside town, in leper colonies. And when they died, the authorities burned their bodies. They burned their clothes, burned their houses and burned everything else they'd ever touched. When lepers walked down the road, they were required by law to warn people of their presence. They were required to scream out, "Unclean! Unclean!"

Do you remember cootie shots in junior high? That's what leprosy was like: the ultimate, fatal cootie. The one unbreakable rule in Jerusalem society in those days was this: You never touched a leper. Can you imagine? Living your entire life without ever being touched? You know what breaks my heart? I think some of you do know what that feels like. At your high school, you feel like a nobody. An outcast. As if there's no one like you. As if you are an untouchable, and when you walk down the halls, people are looking at you as if you are unclean. So, let me tell you what Jesus Christ did with a leper.

Walking down the road, He came upon this leper, a man so overwhelmed by the disease that his eyes were swollen shut and his body bent double. The leper heard the crowd coming, so he yelled out, "Unclean," just as he had a thousand times in his life. Everyone scattered, except one guy, so he yelled it out again: "Unclean!" And still this one man didn't move.

The Bible doesn't explain how the leper knew this was Jesus. It does tell us that the leper fell at His feet and said, *"Jesus, you can heal me if you want to."* Jesus' answer was pretty simple: *"Of course I want to heal you"* (Matthew 8:2-3, paraphrase). And this is my favorite part. Jesus could have healed that guy in a thousand different ways. He could have waved His hand. He could have snapped His fingers. He could have just said it and it would have been so. But Jesus got down in that man's face … and He touched the leper. He touched him. He held his face in His hands. *Jesus Christ. God among us.*

You know what? You are not untouchable. The God of the universe came into this world to touch you. To hold your face in His hands. To wrap Himself around you and squeeze you in an endless embrace. You're not too dirty. You're not too gross to feel His touch. And I want to challenge you to put yourself at the feet of Jesus, whether you know Him or not, and just talk to Him. Remind Him, "Jesus, you can heal me if you want to." And trust me: He wants to.

In John 9, there's another story, a story about a man blind since birth. He is standing before Jesus and he says the same thing: *"You could heal me if you wanted to."* And Jesus does an amazing thing: He spits on the ground. I've always wondered what the blind man was thinking as he heard that spit strike the ground. He recognized the sound. He may have flinched. I'm sure he may have been spit on countless times before. But even as he's thinking this through, Jesus takes the spit and the dirt and makes a little mud pie, which He then rubs on the man's eyes. For a moment, at least, that warm paste hung on his eyelids. The smell of the dirt was in his nostrils. Then he opened his eyes. And he who could not see … saw the face of God.

You know, Jesus takes the ordinary and uses it for extraordinary purposes. I'm living proof. I'm not much to look at. I'm spit. I'm mud. I'm some of the stuff that Jesus takes in His hands and does something wonderful with.

One of my favorite stories in Scripture, in John 8, is about a woman who was a prostitute. Jesus was teaching to a large crowd in a public market. All of a sudden, the religious people, the guys who insisted religion was all about rules and regulations — the exact idea that Jesus turned upside down — dragged this woman into the square. If you've ever seen an aerial picture of Jerusalem on TV and seen that gold dome, that's where Jesus was. And these religious figures and scholars dragged in a woman who'd been caught in the act of adultery. They stood her up in plain sight of everyone. Alone. It takes two people to commit adultery, last time I checked, but this woman was dragged into the square alone.

Waiting for her were the "Pharisees," the guys who made sure people stuck to the rules. Six Pharisees stood there with these rocks and these half-smiles, thinking, "There's going to be a killin' tonight." That's what they did to adulteresses. If a woman had sex with someone who was not her husband in those days, there was no trial. There was no due process. They dragged her to the edge of town. They threw her into a hole. Then everyone in town picked up these huge rocks and chucked 'em at the woman until she died. *"Jesus,"* the Pharisees said, *"this woman was caught in the very act of adultery. Moses' law says she should be killed. Jesus, what do you say?"*

You know what I think? I think it was a set-up, a trap. They wanted Jesus to say something against the religious rules of the day in Jerusalem, so they could try Him for treason. And all the while, this woman was standing there, half-naked. Everyone in the square, especially the men, were trying to sneak a peek. And Jesus? I love this. He stoops down. And He begins to doodle in the dust. He *doodles.* With His finger. In the dust. That *undid* people. The people in the back row are going, "What's He doing down there? What's He writing in the dust?" And all of a sudden, 500 pairs of eyes … are *off the woman.* They were focused, instead, on the God of the universe, doodling in the dust.

Jesus, the Bible tells us, finally stood up. I have to believe He was angry. Righteously angry that everyone in town was belittling this woman. Then He stooped down and doodled in the dust again. And this time when He straightened up, I'd like to think

Jesus snatched a rock away from one of those Pharisees and held it up under his nose. *"Go ahead,"* He said. *"Throw the stone. You be the one. You! You throw it. If one of you has never sinned, you be the first to cast the rock."* Then Jesus stooped and wrote some more.

> *At this, those who heard began to go away one at a time, the older ones first.* John 8:9a (TNIV)

The oldest. The veterans. The old men who'd lived the longest and seen the most knew they'd never seen a man quite like Jesus. The whole square emptied. The woman was left alone. And Jesus spoke to her. *"Hey, where are your accusers? Does no one condemn you?"* He asked. *"No one, Master,"* the woman replied. *"No one is here. No one is here to accuse me." "Neither do I,"* Jesus said. *"Now go on your way. And don't sin anymore."*

God loves sluts. Did you think I was making that up? Jesus didn't come to condemn you. He didn't come to get in your face. He came to save you. Not to condemn, but to save.

I have one last story. There was a woman who'd been hemorrhaging for 12 years. I don't know if it was a menstrual problem, but she had bled consistently for 12 years. She was poor. She didn't have the money to get healed. And she didn't know anything about Jesus. He was on His way to heal a rich man's daughter. The crowd was packed in. Everyone was clustered around Him, like they were trying to get His autograph.

This poor woman figured she had nothing to lose. She didn't know who this guy was, but she saw the crowd and sensed its devotion to Him, and she decided, "If I could just touch Him, maybe I could be healed." So, she reached out. People were shoving her back, but she barely grazed the tip of His garment. Perhaps she snared a tiny string. And immediately she was healed. She could tell. Jesus could tell, too. He stopped. I picture the disciples, banging into each other like dominoes. And Jesus said, *"Who touched me? Who touched me?"* And the disciples said, *"Who touched you? Are you kidding? There's a thousand people in this mob."* But Jesus said, *"No, somebody reached out. I know it"* (Luke 8:45-46, paraphrase).

And somehow the crowd parted, and there was the woman, standing there with this tiny thread. The Bible tells us that Jesus sat and listened to the story of her life. Can you imagine the chat they had that day?

And I wonder: Have you ever tried to talk to Him? If He were passing, would you be curious enough or bold enough to reach out and grab one tiny thread? My promise to you is this: If you do, your life will be changed. Forever. You need to reach out. This is an Amazing Love Story, not a computer chess match where all the moves are programmed in advance. God could have created you to be a robot. He could have programmed you so that you ran around, yelling, "I love God. I love God." But He wanted something better for you. He wanted you to have a choice.

When I was four years old, my father died. He died on the floor of the Anderson, Indiana, jail. Everyone loved my dad. Everybody loved Ernie. He was the town drunk. Two nights earlier, he'd been arrested for vagrancy, for sleeping out on the street. The sheriff's deputies were trying to move him from one cell to another, and he got ornery and someone kicked him, breaking a rib that punctured his lung.

All kinds of things shape us. My father's death obviously shaped me. My mom and my brother and I were left on our own in a tiny, little, one-bedroom apartment. We were dirt poor. There weren't many toys around, which is why I still remember coming out of the house one day and finding on the sidewalk a baby bird.

The bird didn't have any feathers. It was pink and yucky looking, so hungry and thirsty that it just kept opening and closing its mouth. I was sure it was going to die. And I remember thinking, "Here is something that was created to fly — and look at it. It's pitiful." I went inside and said, "Mom! A baby bird!" She said what all moms say about baby birds: "Don't touch it." But of course I went outside and picked it up. My brother and I talked my mom into letting us raise this baby bird. We fed it earthworm shakes and "ladybug delights" and all these nasty things out of an eyedropper. But long after the bird grew feathers and everything else it needed to fly, it would not leave the ground. The bird just sat there. You could walk around the neighborhood with the bird on your shoulder or on the bill of your cap, and it would not fly away. I'd put that bird on the handlebar of my bike and race down the sidewalk, and the bird would just sit there, the wind blowing through its … well, feathers. Finally, my mom got tired of all the things birds do indoors and said, "The bird has to go."

We were bummed, so I, along with all the kids in the neighborhood, started flight training. We decided we'd show the bird how to fly. All my buddies would glide around the yard, flapping their arms. One of them, Randy West, was out in the backyard with two flashlights like the guy at the airport, bringing the bird in for a landing. Nothing. The bird would not fly … until one night I tried to put the bird back in the cage, and without warning, the bird took off like a jet. Inside the house. Up and down the hallways. My mother was hiding behind the couch, clutching the broom like the little guy was a vampire bat or something. My brother went over and opened the front door. All the bird had to do was what he was created to do: Fly. Fly … like a bird. Fly straight through that open door.

You might have thought that little bird was blind. Each time he got close, he'd turn back around. Instead of scooting through the door, he began to fly straight into the huge picture window. He smashed into it headfirst, again and again. Bam! Bam! Bam! Offered an open door, he lunged at that picture window … until the impact finally broke that bird's neck and killed him. He fell down dead on our living room couch. My brother and I walked over to the couch. I looked down at this bird and at 5 years old, I remember thinking to myself, "You stupid bird. All you had to do was go through the door."

Like my pet bird, you and I were created for more than we sometimes realize. Talking about you and me, Jesus said, *"I have come that they might have life, and have it abundantly"* (John 10:10 New American Standard). You were created in the image of God. You were created to fly. Jesus also said this: *"I am the door. If you want to have life, you have to go through Me"* (John 10:9, paraphrase). If you're anything like me, you probably have looked, instead, for life in all the wrong places. You've run headfirst into that picture window in your mad pursuit of power, possessions or popularity. Grades. Sports. Boyfriends and girlfriends. Drugs. Alcohol. Some of those things are really good things, but they have nothing to do with eternal life. They have nothing to do with the reason you were created.

I want you to fly. I want to show you the door and so does Jesus. He was very clear about that. He came so we can have an abundant life. Did He come to open the door? No, much more than that: *"I am the door,"* Jesus said. The door to God. The door to our creator. And no one, Jesus said, "*comes to the Father except through Me"* (John 14:6 TNIV).

Chapter 4
Lobster and Crab Cakes

When I first met my wife, I loved her for more than a year before she even knew I existed. And that was fine. I didn't have any doubts. I wasn't in a hurry. I watched Eva from a distance, waiting until she was at an all-time low so I could make my move. *(Guys: I hope you're taking careful notes.)* Even as I asked her out, I was terrified she'd say no … and surprised when she said yes. I had such big plans. I was thinking marriage before we ever went out. And because I wanted to show her an awesome night, I went out and bought two tickets, center ring, to the Barnum and Bailey Circus. Then I took her to the most expensive restaurant I could afford, which at the time was Red Lobster.

When we got there, she was really down in the dumps. As she scanned the menu, I decided to pave the way for the date and set the tone for this relationship. I wanted her to know she could order anything her heart desired, so I grabbed the menu away from the waiter and said, "I'll have steak and lobster." The most expensive thing in sight. And Eva? She scanned the menu and finally said, "I'd like a crab cake … and a glass of water." A crab cake. A 79-cent crab cake … and a glass of water. I was appalled

… at her loss of appetite and her lack of commitment to this marriage. But that's how it sometimes goes in a love story, even an Amazing Love Story. Some days it's a plate of lobster with that little bowl of butter on the side. And some days it's a lousy 79-cent crab cake and a few crackers. This, now, is the crab cake side of the story I have to tell.

You know, there's a reason we live in a fallen world, a reason why there's cancer, why there's pain, why people beat on us while we were growing up, why our parents get divorced and babies die … and people fly airplanes into buildings. That's what I want to talk about now. It's a message that's hard to receive and a message that's hard to give because it's really bad news. It's the worst news you'll ever hear. And I want to impress upon you that if you walk away from this chapter without the understanding that this is the most devastating, terrible news you've ever heard, then you've missed it completely.

There have been several times in my life when I've been hit with awful news. There was the summer before I started kindergarten. I was sitting on the couch with my mom, totally absorbed in our black-and-white TV set, when she put her arms around me and said that we would never see Daddy again. The town drunk had stumbled into the Anderson, Indiana, jail one last time and he wasn't coming back.

When I was in high school, one of my best friends was a guy named Mike Given. We did everything together. As sophomores, we were together on the gymnastics team. Mike could do back handsprings like no one I've ever seen, up and down the mat. He could knock off 15, 16, 17 in a row, way more than I could do. Each night, we had a contest: Whoever did the most back handsprings didn't have to roll up the mat. Mike always did more than I did. I always got stuck with the tumbling mat. That was understood. But one night, Mike only did 13 handsprings. The next night he did nine, the night after that four or five. Something was wrong. Mike went to the doctor and the doctor told him that what was wrong was leukemia. The doctors figured he would live for another seven years. Seven months later, I walked up and saw one of my best friends lying in a casket.

There's a reason we live in a fallen world. It wasn't that many years ago when another doctor called my wife Eva and me into his office. We were pregnant for the first time. He asked us to sit down. He told Eva that her uterus was heart-shaped, that it had a wall in the middle and that the baby was going to quickly fill up that small space, fooling her body into thinking, much too early, that it was time to deliver. He said we'd probably deliver dead babies several times before we had a live birth. And that was terrible news to a young man who was desperately ready to do the father thing right.

I recognize bad news. I've heard my share. But none of those times compare with the news that I'm going to share with you now. It is hopeless and it is terrifying: Life as you know it is out of whack. You were not created to wither and age … and die. You were created in the Garden of Eden to live forever, in a perfect relationship with a Holy God. You were created by a holy and perfect God to be holy and perfect. You were created in His image. And that was never supposed to change. Listen to the description of the Garden:

At the time God made Earth and Heaven, before any grasses or shrubs had sprouted from the ground … God formed Man out of dirt from the ground and blew into his nostrils the breath of life. The Man came alive — a living soul! Then God planted a garden in Eden, in the east. He put the Man he had just made in it. God made all kinds of trees grow from the ground, trees beautiful to look at and good to eat. Genesis 2:5-9a (The Message)

Everything was beautiful, beautiful beyond description, including a river and a curious tree, the Tree of the Knowledge of Good and Evil. Everything that man and woman needed was provided by God. *Including God. Especially God!* Face to face. God walked with man and woman in the Garden. He came looking for these marvelous new creatures because He loved their company. In the cool of the day, they talked. Adam and Eve beheld the face of God, an opportunity you and I have never had. So, what in the world happened? What happened to change all that was perfect? What happened that made man unrecognizable to God? It was sin.

Now, the serpent was more crafty than any beast in the field.

A love story. Let's not forget thc love story. You were created in the image of God, to love Him and be in a perfect relationship with Him. So were the angels, though the angels were given a choice, just as you are given a choice, of continuing that relationship. One angel chose to live life on his own. He chose to walk backward. He chose to sing a different song, and that had devastating consequences. The serpent, Satan, was a fallen angel. And this serpent made our ol' friend, the Anaconda, seem like a garter snake.

> *The serpent was clever, more clever than any wild animal God had made. He spoke to the Woman: "Do I understand that God told you not to eat from any tree in the garden?" The Woman said to the serpent, "Not at all. We can eat from the trees in the garden. It's only about the tree in the middle of the garden that God said, 'Don't eat from it; don't even touch it or you'll die.'"* Genesis 3:1-3 (The Message)

You have to remember this about the Garden: God provided everything we needed. We were created to enjoy the presence of the God who created us forever. Satan? He brought fear and doubt into Paradise. He tempted Eve with the possibility that this perfect place and this perfect company was only temporary, that it was not designed to last forever. He convinced Adam and Eve that the forbidden fruit — not the perfect God — was their ticket to eternal life. You know the rest of the story.

> *The serpent told the Woman, "You won't die. God knows that the moment you eat from that tree, you'll see what's really going on. You'll be just like God, knowing everything, ranging all the way from good to evil." When the Woman saw that the tree looked like good eating and realized what she would get out*

of it — she'd know everything! — She took and ate the fruit and then gave some to her husband, and he ate. Immediately the two of them did "see what's really going on" — saw themselves naked. They sewed fig leaves together as makeshift clothes for themselves. When they heard the sound of God strolling in the garden in the evening breeze, the Man and his Wife hid in the trees of the garden, hid from God. God called to the Man: "Where are you?"
Genesis 3:4-9 (The Message)

Where … are … you?

God, once again, came looking for those He'd created in His own image. And Adam said, *"I heard the sound of you walking in the garden, O Lord, and I was afraid because I was naked. So I hid myself."*

Imagine that. We went from being in a perfect relationship with God to hiding from Him. And God said, *"Who told you that you were naked? What have you done?"*

We were never meant to go it alone. When we chose to go it alone, to hide from God, to live on the wrong side of the door, it had devastating consequences. Nature was cursed. Pain and suffering arrived. Work — hard labor — became a necessity. Everything changed. God's vision was torn apart. Animals were not created to kill one another. Death was not part of God's grand design. Cancer, sickness and evil came into the world when Adam and Eve chose to take a bite of the one apple that was reserved for God alone.

The Bible is merciless in its description of sin. Romans 3:23 (TNIV) says this: *"For all have sinned and fall short of the glory of God."* First Timothy 2:5 (paraphrase) says this: *"For God is now on one side, and man is on the other."* Can you feel that separation? I do. I feel it every day. I don't feel it the way Adam and Eve did, I suppose. They were wired so that every breath, every thought, their security and their sense of purpose came directly from God. Can you imagine the isolation, the terrible emptiness, when the circuit was broken and they were no longer plugged into their Creator? Perhaps you can.

It's loneliness.

It's looking up into the night sky and feeling unimportant instead of significant.

It's walking past a copy of *Cosmopolitan* magazine and feeling ordinary instead of extraordinary.

It's gazing in the mirror and not meeting a princess or a valiant warrior.

Those are all the consequences of sin. And it doesn't get any worse — or any more brutally honest — than these words in Romans 6:23 (TNIV):

> *For the wages of sin is death.*

Sin, by itself, means you and I are separated from God. Forever. It means we will all die. The bad news, the terrible side of the love story is that sin makes impossible that which we dream about — a relationship with this God who made us and remains among us. Sin makes it impossible for you, on your own, to be in a relationship with the God who created you. Because of sin, you can't do what you were created to do.

And just in case there was some mistake about the sin in our lives, or the possibility that we don't recognize the devastating choices we've made, God gave us the Ten Commandments, a mirror we could hold up to measure the sin on our breath. Because what we *can't* say is that we never took a bite of the apple. I am a liar if I suggest there is no sin in me. What was it that Jesus told the Pharisees, standing in that public square? *"Let he who is without sin cast the first stone."* No one qualified then. No one qualifies now.

If you doubt that, we only need review the Ten Commandments. You can find them in Exodus 20. The first commandment says: *You shall have no other gods before Me.* Place your right hand on the Bible: Is that your story? Is God your knife? If there is anything in your life that is more important than God, you have broken the first commandment.

God is holy. God is perfect. There is no flaw in Him. And the moment there is a flaw in you, you are separated from Him forever. His holiness and our sinfulness do not mix. If you break one commandment, you break them all. And the wages of your sin is death. There is no probation. There is no parole. There isn't a judge on the bench who decides you deserve a lighter sentence. The wages of sin is not just cancer. The wages of sin is not just loneliness … or divorce … or feeling like a nobody. The wages of sin is death. *You shall not make for yourself an idol. You shall not take the name of the Lord your God in vain.* If you've done that once, the wages of sin is death. *Observe the Sabbath and keep it holy. Honor your father and mother as the Lord commanded you. You shall not murder. You shall not commit adultery. You shall not steal. You shall not lie.*

Does anyone feel sinless? Does anyone feel as innocent and pure as the snow that falls on a winter's night? And I am not telling your story. I am telling my story. I am telling our story. No one is righteous before the Lord. Think of the most righteous person you know. The person who loves the Lord the most. Your Young Life leader, perhaps, or the pastor at your church. They are sinners. Just like me. Just like Mother Teresa and Billy Graham. For all have sinned and fall short of God's glory.

I think we need to get on the same page about the nature of sin. Too often we think about sin as the things we do that separate us from God. Things like cussin' and smokin' and cheatin' and lyin' and not honoring your mother and father. Those are sins, true, but they're sins with a little "s."

The sin with the capital "S" is a greater condition. It's a condition we are all born with, as the Apostle Paul tells us in his letter to the Romans. My friend, Mike Given? He had a fatal disease. Leukemia. The symptoms were headaches and nausea. His friends would do things to help him deal with the symptoms of his disease. We'd give him medicine. We'd sneak pizza up to his room so he could catch a break from that hospital chow. But while we were fiddling with the symptoms, the fatal disease remained. That disease took Mike Given to the grave.

You and I waste a lot of time trying to hide the little "s"s in our lives. We make a resolution to get our life together, and for a few hours or a few days, we stop cussin' or stop talking about our friends behind their backs. Or we take the emotional rush we get at some camp experience home with us for a few weeks. But we still all have a fatal disease. It's called Sin. *And the wages of sin is death.*

Death came into the world through the actions of one man and woman, Paul tells the church in Rome … and it has spread to all men and women. It's not that we just make bad choices, though God knows we make plenty of those. We are born with the disease. And that means we are all separated from God forever and we will all die. When you're channel cruisin' on the TV and you run into one of those wide-eyed evangelists and he looks into the camera, shakes his Bible at you and says, "You are a sinner and because of that you're going to hell …" It's the truth. I have too much respect for you to say it that way … but it's the truth. Hell is separation from God. *And the wages of sin is death.*

In the first chapter of Genesis, remember, God looks down on everything He has made and He says, "It is very good." Tove! But, five chapters later His perspective has changed. We are told about that in what may be the saddest verses in the Bible:

> *God saw that human evil was out of control. People thought evil, imagined evil — evil, evil, evil from morning to night. God was sorry that he had made the human race in the first place; it broke his heart. God said, "I'll get rid of my ruined creation, make a clean sweep: people, animals, snakes and bugs, birds — the works. I'm sorry I made them."*
> Genesis 6:5-7 (The Message)

You know, other than Mike Given, my best friend in high school was a dog. Maybe I should be embarrassed to admit that, but hey, you never met this dog. Her name was Tammy. And things seemed so bad at my house that every day when I came home on the bus, I'd go get my gun and my bird dog and we'd disappear together into the woods. I did that to escape. Things were a little rough at home, and Tammy took me away from that.

During my senior year, I somehow scored a date to our winter formal. When that Saturday arrived, I was so nervous that morning that to get rid of the butterflies, I grabbed Tammy and we went out to hunt. We headed to a familiar place, somewhere we'd probably gone together hundreds of times over the years. We were walking along when something set Tammy off and she charged ahead and went over this rise and down into the creek bottom. I didn't yell to her; she'd gone tearing off like this a hundred times before, chasing birds or ghosts or something she sensed and I didn't. But when I cleared the rise and looked over the edge, across this vast valley, Tammy was nowhere to be seen.

I couldn't figure it out. I mean, she was five seconds ahead of me … and then she was gone. At first, I didn't think anything about it. I called her name. She'd always come to me when I called her by name … but this time, she didn't answer. I was sure she could hear me … but she chose not to come to me. She chose not to answer. I stood there, feeling the cold roll in. I stood there, staring out across this lonely, lonely land. There was nothing out there but the echo of that dog's name. That didn't change, no matter how many times I called out to her. She disobeyed. She didn't answer. And because of that, Tammy and I were separated … forever.

Weeping may remain for a night,
but rejoicing comes in the morning.
Psalm 30:5b (TNIV)

After the last chapter, I thought you might need a little consolation from the Psalms. I'm glad you're back. I'm glad you're still reading. Because the Amazing Love Story is about to turn. Morning has broken. The long night is over. And you're about to hear the best news of your life. I can say that with boldness and confidence: I don't think you'll ever forget this message. You won't remember because my signature is on it. You'll remember it because God's signature is all over it.

I've been blessed with good news over the years. Seven months after that first date, that night at the Red Lobster where Eva ordered a crab cake and I took the plunge on the lobster, I took Eva to the next nicest place I could afford. Which means I could only afford to take her there for dessert. I'd arranged for the waiter to let us in at closing time. There was only one other couple in the room when we sat down at a table for two. Inside my sport coat, I had two unused circus tickets from months before in one pocket … and a diamond ring in the other. Eva had no idea what was coming. And when the time finally came, I said this little prayer — "Hi, ho and away we go" — then looked across the table and said, "Eva, I want to spend the rest of my life with you." She just looked at me. Like she had no idea what I was talking about. She didn't realize I was asking her to marry me, and failing miserably. I was starting to panic, so I decided to rephrase the question. "Eva," I said, "I've been thinking about this and praying about this and I want you to be my wife." And because she still didn't say anything, I finally blurted it out as clearly as I possibly could:

"Eva? Will … you … marry … me?"

She was quiet for several seconds; then her eyes filled with tears. She couldn't do anything but nod her head, at which point I jumped up and yelled, "YES!" I got down on my knees and put the ring on her finger, even as this couple — who'd had way too much to drink — stood up and started whoopin' it up. The woman was bawling, saying, "We saw the whole thing!" And the man came swaying over, offering me his hand and saying, "Lemme be da furs to congrajalasha." They were both crying. So was I. I'd never dreamed I'd spend the rest of my life with a princess like Eva.

Another time I got good news was during an evening with Mike Given. Two nights before he died, he asked Jesus Christ to be the Lord and Savior of his life. And I know someday I'll do back flips in heaven with Mike Given.

Good news? Remember that doctor who pulled Eva and me into his office so he could tell us we'd lose a lot of babies? As it turned out, we pumped out four healthy kids like it was nothing. When we were pregnant with our third child, we went to the hospital to get a sonogram. Our two daughters were there. Eva's belly was sticking up off the table about five feet. There was jelly all over her bellybutton and they had this weird camera with the X-ray vision you need to see what's going on with unborn babies. We were looking into this TV screen and in those days, the technology was nothing special, so all we could see was fuzz. We're lookin' and strainin' and trying to find something in the fuzz we recognized when all of a sudden the nurse stopped and yelled, "There! There, do you see it?" I'm looking. I'm smilin'. I'm pretendin' I can see something but I'm drawing a complete blank. Then the nurse goes, "It's a boy!" "I see it!" The girls started giving high-fives.

We danced out into the waiting room and started hugging each other, we were so excited, and there in the waiting room was this grandmother who must have been 190 years old. She had the reading glasses down at the end of her nose and she was literally knitting booties. So, Megan, our youngest, who can barely talk, went over and pulled on her sweater and as this prim, little ol' lady leaned forward, Megan blurted out, "He has a penis!" You bet he does. And that's great news to a guy who never, ever thought he'd have kids.

Remembering those times still brings tears to my eyes. But those stories, those headlines, those bursts of good news don't compare to the glory and the greatness and the wonder of what I'm going to share with you now.

Those are the hors d'oeuvres. That's the crab cake. Now, you're getting lobster. You're about to get the best news you will ever hear in your life. You're getting the punch line of the Amazing Love Story, which is this:

Jesus Christ is your "out" to sin and your "in" to eternal life.

Jesus Christ makes it possible for you to be in a relationship with the God who created you in His image.

Jesus Christ allows you to return to Eden. He pulls you out of hiding so you can have a one-on-one, face-to-face relationship with the God of the universe.

How is Jesus your out? Well, let's begin with the verses I shared with you in the last chapter, the chilling verses that tend to silence all of us. Those verses only tell half the story. They only take us to the edge of the cliff … where God is there to meet us. First Timothy 2:5 begins (and I'm paraphrasing here), *"God is on one side and man is on the other … "* But this is how that verse ends: *"… but Jesus Christ himself is in the middle to mediate, to pull the two together."* Romans 3:23 (TNIV) tells us, *"For all have sinned and fallen short of the glory of God … "* But God doesn't abandon us there. The verse ends, *"… and all are justified freely by his grace through the redemption that came by Christ Jesus."* Romans 5:8 (TNIV) reminds us, *"God demonstrates His own love for us in this: While we were still sinners, Christ died for us."* And in Isaiah 53:6 (The Message), we read: *"We're all like sheep who've wandered off and gotten lost. We've all done our own thing, gone our own way. And God has piled all our sins, everything we've done wrong, on him, on him."*

The sins of the world.

Jesus is your out to sin. He's the only out. He is the only way that the relationship God and man were always intended to have can be restored.

I call this an Amazing Love Story for a number of reasons, and this is surely one of them: Even though we are dealing with a perfect and holy God who could not look upon sin, whose relationship with us was broken by sin, who told us quite clearly that the wages of sin is death, this God somehow stayed involved with us.

From the beginning. Even after kicking Adam and Eve out of the Garden of Eden, He watched over them. Genesis 3:21 says that God provided skins, animal skins, for Adam and Eve to cover themselves. Think about that: That was the first blood sacrifice. That was the first death. Up to that point, death did not exist in Eden. God had not created the plants or the animals, or these two creatures in His own image, to watch them age and crumble and decay. But now, for the first time, God killed an animal so that Adam and Eve could cover themselves.

God stayed involved. He couldn't relate to us the way He had always intended, but He stayed involved. From the beginning, He chose to reveal Himself to sinful man as the God who created them. He sent a flood … but chose a man, Noah, to rise above that flood in his ark. He sent kings, judges, prophets and commandments. He picked a nation, the nation of Israel, as a means to reveal Himself as the door, as the way back into a relationship with Him, as the way to eternal life.

And then He sent Moses.

You've heard of Moses, I'm sure. You've seen *The Prince of Egypt* or, on some Easter weekend when the cable stations roll out the old favorites, Charlton Heston playing Moses in *The Ten Commandments.* You probably remember that Moses parted the Red Sea. But what happened before that, when the Red Sea was still in one piece, is even more important.

In those days, you had an entire nation, the nation of Israel, in slavery. The Israelites couldn't get out of it. Just as you and I are enslaved in sin, desperate for an "out" to escape it, the nation of Israel was trapped in slavery. That's where Moses comes in. God raised up Moses so the nation of Israel would have an "out."

> *God said to Moses and Aaron while still in Egypt, "This month is to be the first month of the year for you."* Exodus 12:1-2 (The Message)

A new beginning. That's what God had planned. That's the promise God was making. Things were never going to be the same from that day forth.

I love that idea. You know why? Because I can make the same promise to you: From this day forth, your life can never be the same. It can never be the same … as a result of what you're going to hear.

The Lord ordered Moses to gather everyone together. He told Moses to instruct each household in Israel to select a lamb:

> *Your lamb must be a healthy male, one year old; you can select it from either the sheep or the goats. Keep*

penned until the fourteenth day of this month, and then slaughter it — the entire community of Israel will do this — at dusk. Then take some of the blood and smear it on the two doorposts and the lintel of the house in which you eat it.
Exodus 12:5-7 (The Message)

And one more thing, the Lord said to Moses:

And here is how you are to eat it: Be fully dressed with your sandals on and your stick in your hand. Eat in a hurry; it's the Passover to God.
Exodus 12:11 (The Message)

To appreciate the significance of the Lord's first Passover, you have to understand two other things: The first is the blood sacrifice. And the second is the long struggle of the nation of Israel to escape slavery.

The blood sacrifice worked like this: If I broke a commandment, I had committed a sin … and the wages of sin is death. I could, however, pay that deadly penalty by killing something else. A dove. A lamb. A bull, if it was a particularly nasty sin. It got fairly ridiculous. Depending on the sin I might have to cut off the head of a turtledove and sprinkle the blood around my head. Or I might have to cut a bull in half — in half! — and walk through the mess seven times. Those were unbelievable times and terribly bloody sacrifices.

And it was just such a blood sacrifice that God finally brought down on Egypt. Moses had been trying to lead the Israelites to freedom for a long time. Because the Egyptian ruler, the Pharaoh, would not let His people go, God had brought all sorts of plagues upon Egypt. One of those plagues was an infestation of frogs. Another time all the dust in Egypt turned into gnats. God even turned the Nile into a river of blood. And when none of that achieved His purpose, God decided He would send the angel of death through the land of Egypt. At each house, at each stop along the way, death would smother the first-born. The first-born calf. The first-born lamb. The first-born child. And, God told Moses, only certain houses would be spared. Only those houses that were marked by the blood of the lamb.

Each house, remember, was "to take a lamb," an unblemished lamb, a year old. They were told to lift that lamb's chin up and slit its throat. As the lamb died, members of the household collected its blood in a bowl. Then they took a small hyssop branch, which was rather like a paint brush, and dipped the branch in the blood. After everyone went inside the house, the father of the household stained the doorposts and the lintel with the blood of the lamb. That blood was so important. That blood was a sign, a sign to God:

> *I will go through the land of Egypt on this night and strike down every firstborn in the land of Egypt, whether human or animal, and bring judgment on all the gods of Egypt. I am GOD. The blood will serve as a sign on the houses where you live. When I*

see the blood I will pass over you — no disaster will touch you when I strike the land of Egypt.
Exodus 12:12-13 (The Message)

This is what happens when a holy and perfect God comes into contact with a sinful man. The wages of sin is death. When God came through town that night, no one was sinless. Everyone deserved to die. But not everyone did. Any family who was inside a house marked by the blood of the lamb got a reprieve. God's wrath and God's judgment passed over them. Was He sparing the sinless? Was He passing over the houses where all the perfect people lived? Of course not. But when He saw the blood of the lamb, His justice, His holiness, His shadow passed over.

In *The Prince of Egypt*, the presence of God is depicted as a fog rolling through town, invading every corner of Egypt … and smothering every first-born except those inside the homes marked by blood. That mark was all that mattered. God wasn't searching the land for the people who were baptized. He wasn't separating the Catholics and the Baptists, the Presbyterians and the Pentecostals or those who went to church from those who didn't go at all. He didn't care if you'd been baptized as a baby, immersed, sprinkled or dunked as an adult ... or done a three and a half off the high dive. He was looking for one thing: the blood of the lamb. That night, as a result of this final plague, Pharaoh finally allowed the Israelites to go, and they escaped slavery, slipping through the Red Sea. And every year, even to this day, the nation of Israel has a Passover feast. As the years went by, God kept revealing Himself through prophets, priests, kings … and that star in the night sky over Bethlehem.

So it was, John tells us in the first chapter of his Gospel, that John the Baptist saw Jesus Christ coming to him.

> *The next day John saw Jesus coming toward him and said, "Look, the Lamb of God, who takes away the sin of the world!"* John 1:29 (TNIV)

Do you see how it works?

Jesus is your Passover lamb.

And when you become a Christian, it doesn't mean that you're never going to sin again. It means that you are symbolically painting the blood of the lamb, Jesus Christ, on the doorposts of your life. Thus, when God looks down on you, He chooses not to see the sin. He sees the blood of the Lamb, sacrificed for you. And His angel of death, His sentence of death, passes over you. As a result, when you die, you won't disappear into the darkness and the dust. Instead, it will be like walking from one room in your house into the next, and immediately finding yourself in the presence of the God who created you, face to face with Jesus Christ. God among us.

How did your Passover lamb die? Well, they didn't lift up His neck and slit His throat. Instead, they hung Him on a tree. The wages of sin is death, remember? God can't get away from that. Somebody has to die. And the Passover Lamb, Jesus Christ, is the sacrifice, once and for all time, for all of your sins, past, present and future.

Then Pilate took Jesus and had him flogged. The soldiers twisted together a crown of thorns and put it on his head. John 19:1-2a (TNIV)

They stripped His clothes off, tied His wrists together and bound Him to what was known as a flogging pole. It was about 6 feet tall and most of you could probably get your arms around it. Now, when it came to handling a whip, the best Roman soldiers knew how to bring someone at the flogging pole to within an inch of their life … or within an inch of their death. They were such pros with the cat o' nine tails — a piece of wood attached to nine leather straps, 6 to 9 feet long, each of which contained pieces of bone, metal and glass — that they could tear a prisoner apart with 40 lashes. Forty lashes at the flogging pole was a death sentence.

Your Passover Lamb, Jesus Christ, received 39.

Then the soldiers spit on Him. They teased Him. They jammed a crown of thorns upon His head. Even Pilate could not slow them down. He came out and said, *"I tell you the truth, I find no guilt in him."* And still the crowd chanted, *"Crucify him, crucify him"* (Mark 15:14, paraphrase). They led Him to Golgotha, the Place of the Skull. It was the day of preparation for Passover. Do you think that it's any coincidence that on the day that Jesus Christ bled and died on the cross, there were thousands of lambs being sacrificed all over Jerusalem?

Golgotha was the city's garbage dump, just outside one city gate. It's called the Place of the Skull because when the sun hits this white, limestone rock face just right, the holes and the shadows appear to be two eye sockets and a mouth. They lay Jesus down on a beam. They put 6-inch metal nails through His wrists. Then they put one foot over the other and nailed both feet to the cross. When Jesus was literally stapled to that cross, they picked it up and dropped that cross into a hole.

Crucifixion was a very common way to execute the enemies of Rome in those days. Most of the time, the dying man's toes were inches off the ground and people would stroll outside the city walls and throw garbage at the prisoner. Death by crucifixion is death by suffocation. Your feet would be in so much pain that you would pull up on your wrists to give them relief. When your wrists screamed in pain, you would push up on your feet. For hours, you would writhe back and forth, while it became harder and harder to breathe. As you hung upon the cross, you lost the strength to lift your body up and allow air into your diaphragm and lungs. If the Roman soldiers ever grew tired of their vigil, waiting for you to die, they'd break your legs so that you couldn't push up at all to get a breath. But they didn't do that to your Passover Lamb.

Jesus hung on the cross for six hours.

At one point during those final hours, Jesus looked up and cried out in a loud voice, *"My God, my God, why have you forsaken me?"* (Matthew 27:46b TNIV). Why would Jesus say something like that? There are 162 times in the Bible where Jesus calls God "Father." Now, suddenly, He addresses Him as "God." Why? Because it was just at that moment that Jesus Christ took on the sins of the world. Your sins. My sins. Sins for all time, past, present and future. And at that point, a holy God could not be in contact with a sinful man. The Holy Father had to break His connection to His Son. Second Corinthians 5:21 (TNIV) says this: *"God made him who had no sin to be sin for us, so that in him we might become the righteousness of God."*

Then Jesus, knowing all things had come to completion, cried out in a loud voice: *"It is finished."* The penalty for sin had been paid.

The Amazing Love Story? It's finished, too. I didn't add anything to it. I haven't taken anything away from it. This is the way it is written. And what's left, I think, is your decision on what you're going to do about it.

> *By his wounds we are healed.* Isaiah 53:5b (TNIV)

You are no cosmic accident. You are fearfully and wonderfully made in the image of a God who is nuts about you. How much does He love you?

> *For God so loved the world that he gave his one and only Son, that whoever believes in him shall not perish but have eternal life.* John 3:16 (TNIV)

I have a favor to ask of you. I'm going to end this chapter with a prayer. And when I say, "Amen," I want you to be absolutely quiet for a few minutes. I want you to put this book down and go somewhere by yourself. It may be the shade of that old tree in your backyard. It may be a corner of your room. But I want you to sit alone and I pray that you will simply ... just be

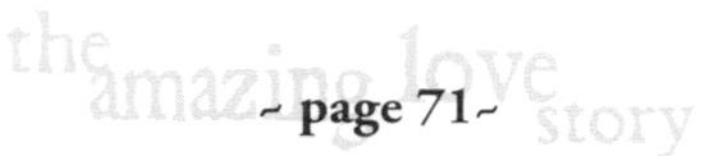

still. I want you to spend some time at the foot of the cross. And I want you to focus on the figure who is hanging there: *God among us.* Maybe you'll want to talk to Him for the very first time ever. Maybe you'll want to tell your whole story to the Lamb of God who took away your sin. Or maybe, in the next few minutes, you'll simply sit quietly and listen as His voice comes searching for you.

> Lord, thank you for the most Amazing Love Story ever told. Thank you for dying on the cross for my sin. I pray now that whether this is the first time or the thousandth time that I've heard this story, that I could spend 15 or 20 minutes with you. That I could imagine what it was like for you that night. That I can spend time at the feet of Jesus, the only place that gives me life.
>
> Amen.

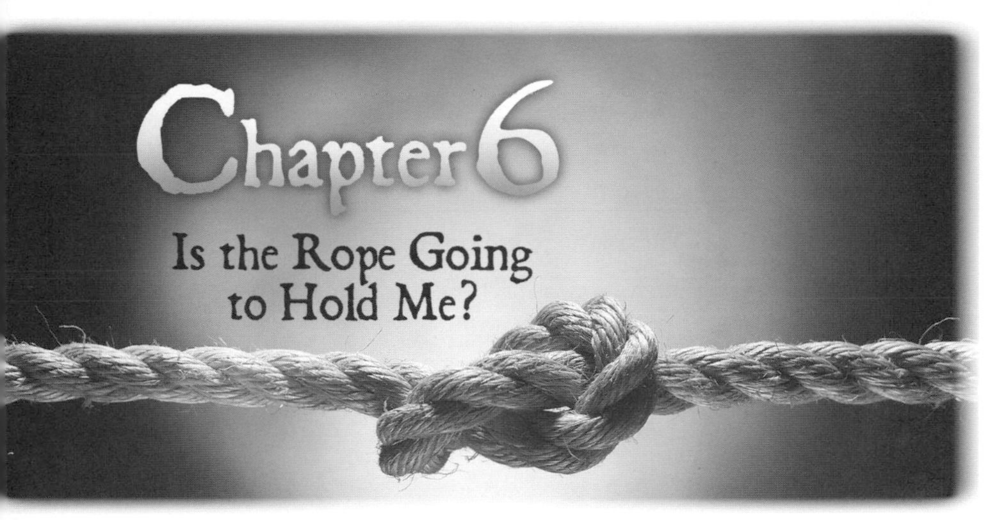

Chapter 6
Is the Rope Going to Hold Me?

He wasn't a victim. You understand that, I hope. As painful as it was for Jesus upon that cross, He wasn't a victim. He was a hero. He is not to be pitied. He chose the cross. He chose to go there for you. He chose to *stay* there for you. Because He was God among us, He could have escaped that agony at any time. But He didn't. He remained on the cross because the wages of sin is death, and He came to die for you and me.

You haven't forgotten Tammy, have you? We went hunting together, remember, that bird dog and me, on the day of my winter formal. And I lost her. Forever. I was angry, confused, crushed that she was gone. Because of Tammy's disobedience, we were separated forever. For hours I called her, again and again, and she didn't answer.

I couldn't stay out there in that field, grieving. I had a date that night. But I did one thing before I left. I took off my winter coat and I laid it on the ground. I left it there in that fallow cornfield.

I'm not going to pretend I had a good time at the dance that night. You know me better than that. As fine as I must have looked in my white, crushed velvet tux, I had a terrible time. And my date picked up on that. At about 10:30 that night, she said, "Hey, it's OK. Leave me here and go look for your dog."

I'll never forget that night. It was the dead of winter and I was heading out into the snow without my coat, just my John Lennon glasses, my platform boots and my shoulder-length hair. When I drove my '71 Chevy pickup onto that field, my lights panned across a fresh bed of snow … And there, asleep on my coat, was my dog, Tammy. Because of one seemingly trivial act, laying my coat down on the cold ground, Tammy and I found one another again.

As special as that reunion was, I wouldn't be bringing it up except that it's a telling metaphor for our reunion with God. Without the act of Jesus Christ dying on the cross, God and man would have been separated forever, too.

It really is an Amazing Love Story. And now you have a choice to make. If I hold out a $100 bill to you, offering it to you as a free gift, when does it become yours? When do you begin to receive the benefits from it? When can you spend it? Only when you reach out … and take it for yourself. That's where we are. Jesus Christ makes God personal, but He'll never force Himself upon you. I want you to count the cost of this decision — the how, the what, the why — even as you decide how you want to respond to the sacrifice He made for you.

Whenever I spend a week at Young Life camp, I always marvel at the drama and the theatrics that take place at the final stage of the ropes course. The ropes course is a series of ladders and bridges, all made of rope, suspended 20 to 30 feet above the ground. It takes guts to maneuver through the course, especially if you're afraid of heights. Even though you wear a harness and a safety line that will break your fall, it's still dicey, particularly at the very end. That's when you're standing on a platform, 30 feet off the ground, facing a trapeze that's hanging just out of reach. Your mission is to stand on the edge of that platform and, with everything you've got, make that desperate leap for the trapeze bar.

I'll be honest with you: Every time I'm on that platform, measuring the distance, getting psyched for that jump, I'm scared to death. But you know what's amazing? While you're waiting, locked into your safety harness, for your turn on the platform, you get to watch 10 or 15 people jump off in front of you. You see the ropes hold them. You see that they do not die. Yet when it's finally your turn, your knees are shaking and your heart is thumpin' and you're thinking, if not screaming out loud, "Is this rope going to hold me?"

You know what? That's where we are right now. Even if you believe the rope is going to hold you, at some point your belief must become faith. You need to act on what you believe. Your feet need to leave the ground. Because the truth is this: You could believe in electricity your entire life, yet live that life in total darkness. You have to believe so much in the power that you can't see that you reach out and flip the switch. You can believe in the Amazing Love Story, believe it to be true, and still not gain the eternal life that it offers to you. Satan recognizes the truth in this story. He's just rejected the choice that you are now facing: To paint the blood of the lamb on the doorposts of your heart.

That's where I come in. I want to show you how to hold the brush. I want to teach you how to become a follower of Christ. I want to teach you how to give your life to Christ, and to accept Him as your Lord and Savior. The whole point of the Amazing Love Story is this: That you would have a personal relationship with the God who created you, through Jesus Christ.

Jesus is the only door. Jesus is our only out.

He's the only way that we can shake free of sin. And if we don't have a personal relationship with Jesus Christ, we remain dead in our sin.

I'm sure some of you are asking: "How can we have a personal relationship with Christ? He's dead! Didn't we leave Him, in the last chapter, hanging on the cross? Didn't He suffer for six hours, cry, 'It is finished' and then die?" Yes. Jesus did all of that. The good news, the great news, of the Gospel is this: Jesus Christ did die. But He's no longer dead. The third day after dying on the cross, He rose from the dead. He came back. Alive. Here's a description of the first Easter in John 20:

> *Early in the morning on the first day of the week, while it was still dark, Mary Magdalene came to the tomb and saw that the stone was moved away from the entrance. She ran at once to Simon Peter and the other disciple, the one Jesus loved, breathlessly panting, "They took the Master from the tomb. We don't know where they've put him."* John 20:1-2 (The Message)

As you can imagine, the two disciples were stunned. They raced to the tomb. When Simon Peter went inside, he *"observed the linen cloths lying there, and the kerchief used to cover his (Jesus') head not lying with the linen cloths but separate, neatly folded by itself."* John 20:7 (The Message)

When Jesus died on that Friday night, His friends took Him down off the cross. Among them was Nicodemus. Do you remember him? He was the guy who was so afraid of what people might think that he went to check Jesus out at night. They didn't waste any time, there at the cross. They brought the body of Jesus down and they wrapped it up like a mummy. Then they put Him inside the tomb. There was a man named Joseph of Arimathea, a wealthy man who offered the friends of Jesus the tomb that was designated for himself. This tomb wasn't a hole in the ground, but a hole in the side of a rock. If you had money, that was a very common way to be buried in those days.

Try to picture that tomb for a moment. Imagine stooping to enter through the doorway. Imagine the flat place, with a stone like a pillow, where they lay the body. I'm asking you to use your imagination because on the day Jesus died, a series of things happened that tested everyone's imagination. He died at three o'clock in the afternoon, we think, and while He was dying, the sky went pitch black. When He cried out, *"It is finished,"* there was an earthquake. And when a Roman soldier pierced Jesus' side with a spear, blood and water gushed out. There was something about His death that caused a Roman centurion, who was guarding the cross, to say, *"Surely, this is the Son of God."* He'd watched it all happen. He'd spent six hours at the Place of the Skull. And after everything he'd seen, he said, *"This has to be the Son of God."*

Do you recognize the feeling? In light of everything we've talked about here, in light of the story I've told?

Not far from Golgotha, there was a temple in Jerusalem which housed the Ark of the Covenant. The ark represented the very presence of God. Do you remember what I told you? When a holy, perfect God comes in contact with sinful man, what happens? Death.

In the temple, the ark was inside a special room called the Holy of Holies. No one could touch the ark or they would die. It was protected by a special curtain that was so heavy that several oxen or mules were needed to lift it up. At the moment Jesus died, that curtain tore in half, from the top to the bottom. God was tearing open the veil that separates us from Him. God was proclaiming to you and me that the debt had been paid, and that sinful man and Holy God could come back into contact with one another, just as they did in the Garden of Eden.

When the disciples returned to find the body of Jesus missing, and the grave clothes undisturbed, the Bible tells us:

> *But Mary stood outside the tomb weeping. As she wept, she knelt to look into the tomb and saw two angels sitting there, dressed in white, one at the head, the other at the foot of where Jesus' body had been laid. They said to her, "Woman, why do you weep?" "They took my Master," she said, "and I don't know where they put him."* John 20:11-13 (The Message)

She walked outside. And Jesus was standing there — alive! — but Mary didn't recognize Him. She thought He was the gardener until Jesus asked Mary the incredible question: *"Mary, why do you look for the living among the dead?"* He called her by name. That was enough. Mary knew that she stood in the presence of the Risen Lord when He spoke her name.

Do you recognize the feeling? Is it possible that for the first time in your life, you feel in your heart and in your bones that God is trying to talk to you?

> *Jesus said, "Mary." Turning to face him, she said in Hebrew, "Rabboni!" meaning "Teacher!" Jesus said, "Don't cling to me, for I have not yet ascended to the Father. Go to my brothers and tell them, 'I ascend to my Father and your Father, my God and your God." Mary Magdalene went, telling the news to the disciples: "I saw the Master!" And she told them everything he said to her.* John 20:16-18 (The Message)

It's an amazing idea, that Jesus could be raised from the dead. But if you have the blood of the Lamb painted on the doorposts of your heart, you will, too.

> *He who believes in Me, though he dies, he will live forever.* John 11:25b (TNIV)

Jesus' triumph over death is more than just a story in the Bible. It's noted in several historical records. A Jewish historian

named Josephus mentions Jesus' life and His death and His resurrection. I understand that you may be wondering about the authenticity of Scripture. You may be asking, "How do I know this is true?" Let me put it this way: Do you believe in George Washington? You do? Why? Because there are written accounts, right? Eye witnesses. Artifacts. Well, there are more written documents, more historical records, that Jesus Christ lived, died and rose again than there are records about the existence of George Washington.

In a letter to his friends in Corinth, Paul talked about the amazing love story that had changed his life (and theirs, too):

> *The first thing I did was place before you what was placed so emphatically before me: that the Messiah died for our sins, exactly as Scripture tells it; that he was buried; that he was raised from death on the third day, again exactly as Scripture says; that he presented himself alive to Peter, then to his closest followers and later to more than five hundred of his followers all at the same time, most of them still around (although a few have since died); that he then spent time with James and the rest of those he commissioned to represent him; and that he finally presented himself alive to me. It was fitting that I bring up the rear. I don't deserve to be included in that inner circle.*
>
> 1 Corinthians 15:3-9a (The Message)

It isn't just a fairy tale, you see. It isn't a daydream. There were eye witnesses who proclaim Jesus rose from the dead. And so can you.

Of the original 12 apostles, all died as martyrs, save one. To escape that death, all they had to do was say that Jesus was not God among us. All they had to do was say it's not true. Instead, they were sawed in half. They were impaled on poles. They were crucified upside down because they didn't think they were worthy to die in the same manner as their Lord.

People aren't willing to die for a lie. Nicodemus. Zacchaeus. Peter. Why, even Nathaniel, who first said, "No, thanks." They all were eventually swept up and blown away by the Amazing Love Story. They all heard the God who created them, walking through the Garden, the garden of their dreams, calling out, "Where are you?" They all decided they no longer had a reason to hide.

Do you?

Sometimes when I would come home from work, when my son Michael was just a little boy, I would bust in the front door and call out, "Michael, where are you? Where are you, Michael?" I'd look behind the sofa. I'd look behind the fica tree we had by our picture window. I'd look behind the drapes. All of which was ridiculous because Michael couldn't hide worth a lick. Michael would lie down on the living room floor and put the blankie over his face while his big ol' naked belly would be sticking out. I'd be crawling over him, going, "Michael, where are you?" and the blankie would be shaking because he'd be laughing so hard. I'd go wandering into the next room to make my voice seem far away, and that drove him crazy! That's when I'd hear him say: "Here I am, Daddy!" Because, you see, while Michael liked to hide, he loved to be found.

My son doesn't know all the books in the Bible. He can't comment on the Gnosis passage of Philippians 2. I don't think he knows the first thing about the seven dispensations of Revelation. But he knows how to paint the blood of the Lamb on the doorposts of his heart. It's as easy as "A-B-C," he'll tell you.

A? Admit. Admit you're a sinner. Admit you're far away from God. Admit that the wages of sin is death.

B? Believe. Believe Jesus is your Passover Lamb. And that the wages of sin have been paid by Christ's death on the cross.

C? Commit. Accept Jesus as not only your Savior, but your Lord. The boss of your life. Commit that from this day forth, you're going to try to be more like Jesus, every single day.

Do you want to pick up that brush? Are you ready to dip it in the blood? I don't care whether it's five minutes from now or five days or five weeks. All you need to do is look up into the night sky and say, "Here I am, Daddy." God knows what you need. You don't even have to get the words right.

I still remember the time I told this story and this guy came busting in after being wrestled to the ground by the idea that Jesus died for him. "Ash," he said. "I want to become a Christian. I want to paint the blood of the Lamb on the doorposts of my heart." "John, that's great," I said. "You wanna do it right now? C'mon, let's do it. Let's say the A-B-C prayer together."

We're sitting on two chairs, face to face. I had his hands in mine. I said, "Okay, John, go ahead." I waited a long time for John to pray … but there was just silence. I finally opened one eye to check on John and he's looking back at me with one eye, more than a little lost. "How about if I say the 'A' part of the prayer, the 'Admit' part?" I said. "We can do that?" John said. "That's legal?" "Sure," I said. So, I prayed the A part: "Lord, I admit I'm a sinner." Then I waited for John to jump all over the B part … but there was nothing. I slid open that one eye again, and John is looking back at me with his one eye and he says, "Ditto." And so it was that John from Horseshoe Bend, Idaho, accepted Jesus Christ as his Lord and Savior by saying, "Ditto," about five times.

You have to understand this: God does not play games with you. He doesn't say, "C'mon, fall in love with me. Closer … closer … missionary to Africa!" He's not like that. Remember? He's crazy about you. There's nothing you've ever done that would make Him want to stay away from you. Just say, "Ditto." Say, "Here I am." Say, "A-B-C." He knows what you need. He'll get the message.

Back in the days when Jesus was trudging through the dust of Palestine, He had a friend named Lazarus. His friend died. And when Jesus got to the place where they'd buried him, four days later, Martha came running up to Him and said, *"Jesus, if only you had been here, my brother would not have died."* And Jesus said, *"Your brother will be raised up." "I know he will be raised up on the last day,"* Martha said. But Jesus answered, *"You don't have to wait until the end. I am the way, the truth and the life. Do you believe this?"* (John 11:21-26, paraphrase). That's the question, isn't it? Do you? Somehow, our belief must become faith. You have to believe in it so much that you act on it.

Standing outside the tomb where Lazarus was buried, Jesus said, *"Roll away the stone."* Everyone got a little indignant. The guy had been rotting there for days. They didn't even want to think about the smell hiding behind that stone. But I think Jesus nailed it. The first step to painting the blood of the Lamb on the doorposts of your heart is to roll away the stone and expose the stink of your life to Jesus Christ.

"I say this prayer," Jesus said, *"so that everyone will know you are God."* Then He said, *"Lazarus come forth"* (John 11:41-43, paraphrase). As everyone stared into the black pitch of the grave, Jesus called Lazarus by name, just as He would call Mary by name outside another tomb. And Lazarus? I don't know if he limped out of that tomb or floated up out of the darkness. But he rose. He returned from death to life.

Lazarus, come forth! Christina? Your name is on Jesus' lips. Come forth. Larry? Ivan? Ben? Kendra? Come forth. Keisha? Rob? Kevin? Julio? I wish I could call all of you by name. Because Christ wants to bring you all out of hiding. Christ invites you all back to life and into a relationship with Him.

How does your belief become faith?

A long time ago, I was putting a roof on my house … and keeping an eye out for my daughter, Melissa. She was barely old enough to walk a straight line. There was no way, I didn't think, she could get in much trouble. But when I walked inside to get a drink of water, I came back outside to find Melissa on the roof.

She was standing in the gutter. She had one hand on the ladder and she was grinning down at me. I looked at her and I knew we were in big trouble. So I put a big, clumsy smile on my face and started up that ladder to rescue my little girl. Melissa thought this was a marvelous game. She took off running along the edge of the roof. So I stopped … and she stopped. When I came down the ladder, she came back to the top. And I realized it was going to take something radical to get her down. I stepped away from the ladder, looked her right in the eye, and said, "Melissa? Jump!"

Melissa? She believed. She believed with all her heart that her daddy would catch her. But her belief became faith when her feet left the roof.

It wasn't a mature, intellectual leap. It was innocent, childlike faith. It's the only kind of faith the Bible talks about. I love my little girl. I'd never let her hit the ground. And your Heavenly Father loves you so much more.

So, there are you are. On the edge of the roof. And your loving Father is calling your name and asking you to leap. For that trapeze bar that is hope and eternal life with Him. He's not going to force you. He's not going to send a fearsome wind along the eaves. What makes this a love story, an Amazing Love Story, is that He offers us a choice. A choice. A lamb. And a place to land.

Chapter 7

He Who Has the Son Has Life

I never know how to close. I never know what to say when I reach the end of the Amazing Love Story. So let me begin like this: I have tried, above all, to speak the truth, the truth about one who loves you and loves you the most — Jesus Christ. *God among us.* God's logo. The word made flesh among men.

When you began this book, I made you a deal — that I would tell you the story the best I could and that the way you responded would be completely up to you, with no strings attached. I hope you jumped in with both feet. I hope that somewhere in the middle of these pages, you stopped, shaken by God's love for you, and gave your life to Christ. I rejoice with you.

But I also know that you may have heard the Amazing Love Story and you're not ready for that kind of commitment, or you just don't buy into it, just as Nathaniel didn't in the beginning. I want you to know that doesn't change some things. I still love you. More importantly, God still loves you. He's nuts about you. He is the God who created you and nothing will ever change that.

I also want you to understand that you have not missed a

once-in-a-lifetime opportunity. God is not just in these pages. He's everywhere. He will go with you when you put this book aside. What's more, you know everything you need to know to give your life to Jesus Christ. From this day forth, all you need to do to become a Christian is to look up into that night sky and say: "Here I am, Daddy." Maybe when that time comes, you'll be so caught up in the moment that nothing will come out of your mouth except, "Ditto. Ditto. Ditto." Maybe, in your mind, you'll jump off the roof, into the hands of an awaiting Savior. Or maybe, just maybe, late at night, when no one is around, you'll whisper the A-B-C prayer. Admit. Believe. Commit. I'm going to write the words down for you, so you'll always have them. And I'd be honored, and humbled, if — now or somewhere around the bend — you would pray along with me:

> Dear Lord, I admit to you that I'm a sinner. I'm so, so sorry that I've lived life on my own. I know I was never created to go it alone. I was created to be in a relationship with you.
>
> Lord Jesus, please forgive my sins. Lord, I believe that you died on the cross for my sins. I know that the wages of sin is death, and that Your death bought me back. Your death was my "out" to sin.
>
> Lord, I commit. I accept you as my Lord and Savior. I commit my life to you. From this day forth, I promise you I'll try to be more like you every day.

I symbolically paint the blood of the Lamb on the doorposts of my heart. And I thank you for the promise that you'll never look at me the same way again.

In your name I pray.
Amen.

Just like that, you take a step … from death to life. If you have given your life to Christ, I want to remind you that you may be about to hit the wall. Outside the boundaries of this book are situations at home that aren't ideal for someone who is about to take their first baby steps in their relationship with God. Your walk with Christ is not a feeling. It's a relationship.

Almost 25 years ago, I stood before a congregation of people and took vows of marriage with Eva. On that day, before God and people who loved me, I set my life aside for Eva. I gave myself to her as a husband and I took her as my wife. What binds us together are those vows. There have been a lot of days in the last 20 years, including the mornings when we wake up and blow bad breath on one another, that we don't feel very married. But we are. Nothing can take that away.

What makes you a Christian — one with Christ — is your understanding and your vow and your commitment to Christ as your Savior. There are a lot of days when I don't feel very Christian, and there will be a lot of days when you don't, either. But I am. And you are. Christ promised you He would never leave you. The last thing He said before He ascended into heaven was, *"And surely I am with you always, to the very end of the age"* (Matthew 28:20 TNIV). He will never leave you. You will never be without Christ. The Gospel of Mark describes new Christians as being in God's hands, and nothing can snatch you away. That's exactly what Paul meant when he wrote:

> *For I am convinced that neither death nor life, neither angels nor demons, neither the present nor the future, nor any powers, neither height nor depth, nor anything else in all creation, will be able to separate us from the love of God that is in Christ Jesus our Lord.* Romans 8:38-39 (TNIV)

Nothing, nothing, nothing, can separate you from the love of God. Does that mean you're going to do "better," that armed with the love of God you're going to automatically clean up your act? Well, I gotta tell you: Christianity is not about being better. It's not about doing good. It's a relationship. You are going to sin again, and it's going to make you feel guilty. That's good! Before Christ comes into our lives, there's not that much conviction. But that guilt won't mean that Christ has left you. Christianity is not rules. It's not regulations. It isn't feelings. It isn't doing better. It's a relationship.

How silly it would have been for me, on my wedding day, to look in Eva's eyes, to take her as my wife, to kiss her, then turn around, give her a high five and say, "This marriage thing is great, I'll see you on my death bed." I love Eva. It's a love story. It's a relationship. And I want to cultivate my relationship with Eva every single day. That's why I'm begging you to cultivate your friendship with Jesus Christ.

No matter where you are in your relationship with Jesus — if you've been a Christian for years or you just gave your life to Jesus — read your Bible every day. Any Bible. Any translation. In the last quarter of the Bible, the New Testament, you'll find the books of Matthew, Mark, Luke and John. That's the Amazing Love Story. It's the same story told by four eye witnesses. Start in the Gospel of Mark. It's the shortest. It's the *CliffsNotes* version of the Amazing Love Story. But read it. Right before you go to bed, if that's the only time you have. Don't go to sleep without reading a paragraph.

Another thing I want to encourage you to do is to go to church. I know you may not have real positive feelings about church. I can relate. I used to not like church, either. Even now, I only go to church 30 or 35 times a year because I travel so much. And so many times, it's only an OK experience. I'm asking myself, "Why am I here today?" But my attitude toward church changed when I discovered, in the Amazing Love Story, that I don't go to church to get anything. I go to church to give everything. I go to church for everybody sitting around me. If there are people behind me not smiling, I'm grinnin' at 'em. I go to give worship to my Lord. So, go to church. Go to give to God. If your family has any connection to a church, start there. If you have no connection at all, go to the church of your Young Life leader or a friend you look up to.

And if your family goes to a Catholic church, that's great. The beautiful traditions and terminology of your church are not quite the same as I am using in this book. Don't worry about that. It's the same Amazing Love Story. This is what you might want to tell your priest. Tell him that you heard the Amazing Love Story and you finally understand your confirmation. You gave your life to Christ. Then ask him, "How can I help you spread the Amazing Love Story in your church?" When he hears that, I'm betting your priest may pass out with joy!

Other than reading the Bible and going to church, I want to encourage you to pray every day. And for those of you who've been a Christian for a long, long time, I want to beg you to stop being such a lightweight with your faith. Do you realize that Christ is counting on you? There are lepers in the hallways of your school. There are hemorrhaging women who are reaching out, desperately, to get one touch of Jesus Christ. There are snakes coming after people you love, determined to squeeze them until they die and swallow them whole.

When you become a Christ One, when you paint the blood of the Lamb on the doorposts of your heart, Jesus sends His Holy Spirit upon you. And now you are the visible expression of an unseen God. You are the word made flesh among men. Don't you know your job description? You're spit. You're mud. You're a thread. You're foot water … that Jesus Christ can turn into a miracle! So, I beg you to get off your fanny. Get off the roof. Get in the game.

First Corinthians 3:16 (TNIV) says this: *"Don't you know that you yourselves are God's temple and that God's Spirit dwells in your midst?"* God doesn't want you on the sidelines. God needs you in the game, so that He can work through you. In your cafeteria, at your school, I hope no one ever sits by themselves again. I hope no one ever walks the halls, feeling unloved and unclean. I hope no one ever comes to you with a hyssop branch and finds your bucket empty. Christ is counting on you. I also want you to feel secure in your salvation. He's got you! Listen to this story in Matthew 14:

> *As soon as the meal was finished, he insisted that the disciples get in the boat and go on ahead to the other side while he dismissed the people. With the crowd dispersed, he climbed the mountain so he could be by himself and pray. He stayed there alone, late into the night. Meanwhile, the boat was far out to sea when the wind came up against them and they were battered by the waves. At about four o'clock in the morning, Jesus came toward them walking on the water.* Matthew 14:22-25 (The Message)

Now, this boat couldn't have been bigger than a couple big ol' couches strapped together, with one mast going up the middle. The waves were coming over the side, and all the disciples were terrified, just like they were in the story I told you at the beginning of this book. They were yelling at each other, and the wind was howling right along with them. And Jesus came along, walking on the water. And the first thing they screamed was, *"It's a ghost!"* They were scared out of their wits.

> *But Jesus was quick to comfort them.*
> Matthew 14:27a (The Message)

Hey. Cry out. In your terror. Jesus is quick to comfort you. You'll never be alone again.

> *"But Jesus immediately said to them, 'Take courage! It is I. Don't be afraid.' 'Lord, if it's you,' Peter replied, 'tell me to come to you on the water.'"*
> Matthew 14:27-28 (TNIV)

And Jesus looked at Peter and said, *"Come on."* Peter looked back at his disciple buddies and they said, *"Go ahead."* They couldn't wait to see how this was going to turn out. So, Peter stepped out of the boat. He stepped out. Hebrews 2 talks about fixing your eyes on Jesus. That's what Peter did, at least at first. And he was fine. He was walking on water until he took his eyes off Christ. He looked at the waves and that's when he began to sink.

I know the feeling. I lose sight of Jesus, the author and perfector of our faith, and I am swallowed up by the waves and the turmoil around me. But here's what Peter does: He cries out. *"Master! Save me!"* And Jesus? He didn't hesitate. He reached out … and waved goodbye as Peter sank to his death … you think? No, He reached out and grabbed his hand and said, *"Hey, Peter, what got into you?"*

Jesus is not going to let you sink. Cry out to Him … and He will rescue you. "Master! Save me!" "Melissa! Jump!" He will never let you down.

I want to close with a story that's not part of the Amazing Love Story and it's not a story in the Bible. I don't even know the source of the story. I wish I did because it summarizes the message I want you to take from this book.

Near the end of World War I, there was a world-renown artist living in Europe. He was the lucky artist who became famous while he was still alive. Everyone wanted his paintings. He lived way up in the mountains, in his tiny cabin studio. He drew pictures of the mountains and sunsets. He loved to paint God's creation. The only thing he cared about more was his only son, the son who, as the story goes, was sent off to fight in the Great War.

Months passed and there came a knock upon the door. When the artist answered it, two soldiers were standing there in military honor dress and holding a shoebox. The box held the son's personal effects, the last, lingering images of a boy who'd been killed in battle. The artist took the shoebox back into his cabin. He set the box aside without opening it and he grieved. He grieved terribly over the loss of his son. He stopped painting completely and became a recluse. He never left his cabin again. And those who knew him were convinced that he would never paint again.

About a year later, late at night, accompanied by nothing other than the dim light of a candle, the artist reached over and picked up the box, and opened it. He found trinkets, buttons, medals. But at the bottom of the box, the old man found a piece of paper, folded four times. When he opened it up, he discovered a picture of his son's face. A self-portrait. Somewhere in Europe, in the bottom of the trenches and the belly of the war, his son had gotten hold of a piece of paper and a piece of charcoal and made a crude sketch of his own face. The artist moved aside the masterpieces sitting atop the mantle over his fireplace. He placed the picture of his son in the most prominent place in his home. It became his prize possession.

A few years passed and the artist died. When a huge auction of his work was announced, the art world got excited. Every stunning masterpiece in his personal collection was available and millionaires and art dealers arrived at the auction house from around the world. Everyone had their checkbooks out when the auctioneer stepped forward and said, "Let the auction begin." A curtain opened. And there on the easel was that charcoal sketch of the artist's son. Several people began to boo. "We didn't come here for that," they yelled. "We want the good stuff. We came to buy the masterpieces." The auctioneer was a little embarrassed. He flipped through his papers and he said, "No, please, the artist made it perfectly clear that the picture of the son goes first. Again, let the auction begin!"

No one would bid on the charcoal sketch. There was a long, awkward silence until finally, one frail, old man in the back row, a friend of the artist, a virtual town beggar, raised his hand and said in a gentle voice, "I'll give eight dollars. It's all I have." The auctioneer looked out over the crowd, somewhat surprised, somewhat relieved. "Eight dollars, going once," he said. "Eight dollars, going twice. Sold! To the man in the back row for eight dollars." Then the people began to mumble again, even as the old man worked his way through the crowd to the stage, tucked the picture of the artist's son under his arm and began to wander off. No one paid him any mind. Everyone else was ready for the master's works.

That's when the auctioneer picked up his hammer again and announced, "The auction is closed!" There was pandemonium on the auction floor. Everyone freaked out. They were indignant. Closed? What was he talking about? The auction was just getting started. But the auctioneer said, "No. The artist made it perfectly clear. He who takes the son takes it all!"

Mark 4:41 says (and I'm paraphrasing here), "*'Who is this Jesus,' the disciples asked, 'that even the wind and the sea obey Him?'*"

I'll tell you who He is. He is God. Jesus is God. And as 1 John 5:12 (TNIV) reminds us:

> *Whoever has the Son has life; whoever does not have the Son of God does not have life.*

Dear friend, you were created to fly. I beg you on behalf of Christ to be reconciled to God … and to go through the door of Jesus Christ.

Mike "Ash" Ashburn

Mike "Ash" Ashburn lives in Fishers, Ind. He is father to four: Melissa, Megan, Morgan and Michael and husband to one ... Eva. One dog, two cats and two lizards currently complete their home. Ash enjoys hunting, fishing, frog gigging and most things outdoors. His favorite thing to do is be with his family!

Ash has been affiliated with Young Life* for more than 30 years. He served as a volunteer leader, staff trainee and was area director in Anderson, Evansville, Newburgh, Ind., and Roanoke, Va. Since 1995, Ash has served Young Life as the special assistant to the president. In this capacity Ash shares his gifts as a performing artist, speaker, musician and humorist all over the world. Still, his favorite assignment is spending a month each summer at Young Life camps sharing this "amazing love story" with teenagers.

Ash has a B.S. in Forestry from Purdue University, with a major in wildlife management. He says he still manages wildlife (Young Life kids as well as his own). He is an ordained evangelist with the Evangelical Church Alliance and has an M.A. in Theology and Youth Studies from Fuller Seminary.

Rev. Mike "Ash" Ashburn is also the founder and president of Gospel Seed Productions*, which has served as another vehicle to produce a stage play called the *Whittlin' Man*, and a video on teenage abstinence called *Let's Talk About It.*

**For more information about Young Life, visit www.younglife.org. For more information about booking Ash for an engagement, contact evava@aol.com or call 1-800-341-9902.*

Steve Duin

Steve Duin writes the Metro column for *The Oregonian* in Portland, Ore. He first heard "The Amazing Love Story" at Young Life's Malibu Club in the summer of 1972 and has remained a devoted fan of the ministry ever since. Duin has co-authored a history of comic books and a retrospective on space toys; *Father Time*, a collection of columns on his odyssey as a parent, was published in June 2005. He lives with his wife and three children in Lake Oswego, Ore.